TOP 10 WINES
AUSTRALIA &
NEW ZEALAND

TOP 10 WINE
SELECTIONS BY
VINCENT GASNIER

Contents

Left **Cellars at Kumeu River Wine, New Zealand** Right **The Yarra Valley in Victoria**

LONDON, NEW YORK,
MELBOURNE, MUNICH AND DELHI
www.dk.com

First American Edition, 2006

Produced by Blue Island Publishing,
Studio 218, 30 Great Guildford Street, London SE1 0HS, UK

First published in the United States by
DK Publishing, 375 Hudson Street
New York, NY 10014

06 07 08 09 10   10 9 8 7 6 5 4 3 2 1

**Based on Wines of the World, first published
by Dorling Kindersley 2004
This compilation © 2006 Dorling Kindersley Limited**

A Cataloging-in-Publication record for this book is available from
the Library of Congress.

ISBN-10: 0-7566-2256-5
ISBN-13: 978-0-7566-2256-5

DK books are available at special discounts for bulk purchases for sales
promotions, premiums, fund-raising, or educational use. For details, contact:
DK Publishing Special Markets, 375 Hudson Street, New York, NY 10014
or SpecialSales@dk.com

Color reproduction by Colourscan, Singapore
Printed and bound in China by Leo

Discover more at www.dk.com

Every effort has been made to ensure that this book is as up-to-date as possible at
the time of going to press. Some details, however, such as telephone numbers, website
addresses, and wine label names are liable to change. The publishers cannot accept
responsibility for any consequences arising from the use of this book, nor for any
material on third party websites, and cannot guarantee that any website address in this book
will be a suitable source of information. Please address any queries to DK Publishing.

Left **Tahbilk Winery** Center **Leeuwin Estates label** Right **Cloudy Bay bottles**

Contents

Rippon Valley on Lake Wanaka, New Zealand

Key to Symbols Used in Book

- ▨ soil types
- 🍇 red grape varieties
- 🍇 white grape varieties
- 🍷 wine styles
- ✆ contact details
- ☐ open to the public
- ⬤ not open to the public
- ★ notable wine brands or varietals

The World of Wine

Wine is as simple or as complex as you wish: on one level, it can be an immediate sensory pleasure, or, at a deeper level, the embodiment of a piece of land and a moment in time. Wine is a pure reflection of its terroir (see opposite) and no other product expresses its cultural and geographical origins in quite the same way. Each harvest yields wines that are the culmination of different climatic and human processes, so no two wines are ever identical.

Origins and Cultural Significance of Wine

Bacchus, painted by Caravaggio (c.1593)

Wine is thought to have originated in the Caucasus mountains of Georgia and it has been part of world culture since historical records began. In ancient Greece and Rome, the god Dionysus (or Bacchus) embodied the spirit of celebration with wine. Firmly established as part of the Mediterranean way of life, wine subsequently became an important part of the Christian religion. In the Middle Ages European monasteries did much to advance the quality of wine, improving vine cultivation and developing new winemaking techniques in their cellars.

As Europeans ventured into the New World from the 16th century onward, their religion and their vines went with them. Being clean and safer to drink than water, wine became as much a part of daily life for slaking thirst as it was a major sacramental tradition.

Over the centuries, wine trading burgeoned, bottlemaking techniques were perfected, sparkling winemaking evolved, and fine wines became highly prized. The wine world as we know it began to take shape.

Today, more than ever, wine is a part of everyday life throughout the world, both as a celebratory drink and as a versatile partner to food. That it has become so intrinsic to world culture is hardly surprising. Aside from the relaxing effects of alcohol, wine continues to fascinate with its ever-changing character, so inextricably linked to the land, people, and culture that created it.

Vineyard in the Margaret River wine region of Western Australia

Wine Regions of the World

At the beginning of the 21st century, the world has more than 19 million acres under vine and is producing nearly 237 billion gallons of wine each year. Vineyards are concentrated between 32° and 51° in the northern hemisphere, and between 28° and 42° in the southern. Wine is now made in virtually all parts of the world that enjoy a suitable climate—from Chile to New Zealand and from South Africa to China. France is the biggest producer, followed by Italy, Spain, the US, and Australia.

While the classic wine regions of Bordeaux, Burgundy, the Rhône Valley, Rioja, and Tuscany have a long-established status as the global benchmarks for fine wine, it is the pursuit of new *terroir* that has led growers to venture into viticulturally unexplored corners of Europe and into the New World. Many of the newfound lands in Australasia and the Americas have proved easy vineyard territory, where grapes can grow in the heat with little apparent effort. But more and more, producers have found that the best wines come from vineyards where heat is tempered by the soothing

What is Terroir?

In every vineyard, a unique combination of climate, topography, and soil type shapes the character of the vines that grow there. Rich soils can lead to excessive leaf growth and mediocre fruit. Soils of low fertility are therefore better. Soil structure is considered even more important than chemical make-up, with good drainage being essential. The grapes that the vines yield and, in turn, the wine made from these grapes reflect aspects of this distinct place. The French word *terroir*, literally meaning "soil," is used to describe not only the soil, but the entire environment in which the vine grows. Find the right *terroir* and the resulting wines will have the most harmonious composition with acidity, sweetness, fruit flavors, and tannins, all poised to perfection. With the wrong *terroir*, the harvest will all too often fail.

effects of water—a lake, river, or coastline—or the cooling influence of altitude. Emerging wine areas such as the island of Tasmania in Australia are proving themselves in this respect. When the vines have to work that bit harder to survive, grapes tend to develop more refined flavors.

For more general information about wine, including styles, tasting terminology, and a glossary, **See pp136–153**

Old versus New Wines

Today, wine is said to come from the Old World or the New. The classic regions of France, Italy, and Spain are at the core of the Old World. The New World comprises the southern hemisphere and North America. Until recently, it was relatively easy to pick up a glass of wine and identify, with a small sniff and a sip, whether it was from the New World or the Old. A New World wine would have all the rich fruit flavors and aromas that reflect warm-climate vineyards. An Old World example would be more subtle with delicate, complex aromas and leaner flavors. Today, however, improved techniques mean that an Old World wine can taste as luscious and ripe as a New World version. Meanwhile, the New World is busy using Old World techniques such as barrel-fermenting, wild yeasts, and lees-stirring to create more complexity.

Estate versus Branded Wines

Techniques in the winery are now so advanced that, with recourse to appropriate grapes, a winemaker has many options. The art of making the mass-production wines is to make each batch and vintage the same so that the brand is reliable and affordable. Estate wines, by contrast, are a true reflection of their land and culture. These are the wines that evoke passionate discussion, genuine loyalty—and a hugely variable price range. They are also the wines that can undergo near-miraculous flavor transformations when laid down to age.

Trends in Wine Consumption

The traditional wine-drinking countries of France, Italy, and Spain have actually seen a slump in consumption over the last 30 years. There are several reasons for this. In the first place, because water quality has improved, wine is no longer needed as a general beverage, and it is perceived as an impediment to work performance. There has also been a decline in café drinking. In an effort to combat the ever-growing European "wine lake," wine is thus produced in smaller quantities and to a higher standard (and price) in these countries. It is no longer regarded as a drink for quaffing, but for sipping and enjoying.

In the English-speaking world, the picture is quite different; wine consumption in the UK, for example, has risen by over 500 percent since 1970. The surge in wine's popularity is a direct result of the huge quantities of affordable ripe-fruited New World wines flooding onto the market and the advent of "branded" wines. Wine is no longer the preserve of a wealthy elite.

There is a general belief that wine is part of healthy living. Wine's benefits as a sociable beverage, a health-giver, and an all-round focus of interest suggest it will be part of culture for years to come.

Huia Vineyards, Marlborough, New Zealand

Vincent Gasnier

"It always gives me great pleasure when I can pass on what I have learnt from tasting many of the world's finest—and not so fine—wines in a simple, easily-assimilated form. So I was delighted when Dorling Kindersley invited me to provide lists of the Top 10 Wines of Australia and New Zealand, category by category. Obviously there was not room to include every deserving wine, but the lists have been devised to cover a broad range. They naturally feature many well-known labels from major producers, but they also contain lesser-known wines from talented, up-and-coming winemakers."

Vincent Gasnier
London, May 2006

TOP 10 Selections
No hierarchy of quality is implied by the order in which the wines appear in the Top 10 lists. The 10 selections are of roughly equal merit.

About Vincent Gasnier

A young French sommelier, now working in Britain, Vincent Gasnier has enjoyed a rapid rise to preeminence in his profession. In 1994–5, while working at the Restaurant Laurent, on the Champs-Élysées in Paris, he was promoted to Sommelier under Philippe Bourguignon, regarded as one of the best sommeliers in France. In 1997, at the age of 22, he qualified as Master Sommelier: the youngest person in the world to achieve this distinction. After a period as Chef-Sommelier at the Hotel du Vin, Winchester, he set up in business for himself. Since August 2000 he has been Managing Director of Vincent Gasnier Wine Consultant Limited, offering advice on wine purchase, cellar management, VIP wine events, and exclusive wine tours. He shares his expertise with many distinguished individual and corporate clients, including the Houses of Parliament in London. He is a wine judge and has appeared on TV and in magazines.

For more on Vincent Gasnier, check **www.vincentgasnier.co.uk**

WINES OF AUSTRALIA

Introducing Australian Wine

Australia is one of the great success stories of the New World of wine. This is a country that has broken free from the traditions and rules of the Old World. It is technologically innovative, consumer-oriented, internationally competitive, and, above all, it produces reliably sun-drenched, fruit-driven wines. In recent years, Australia has risen to become the world's fourth largest exporter of wine.

Early Years

The first governor of New South Wales, Arthur Phillip, who landed at Sydney Cove in 1788, is said to have planted Australia's first grapevine in his garden. Other pioneers made attempts at producing wine, but it was not until 1831, when James Busby, an energetic Scot, collected some 543 different vines from Europe (of which 362 survived the voyage) that winegrowing really took off. Busby had the vines planted in Sydney's Botanic Gardens, and cuttings from them provided the basis of the country's wine industry.

Governor Arthur Phillip

In the early 19th century, the wine industry was dominated by British-born landed gentry who had settled in New South Wales, Victoria, and South Australia. Key figures with enduring names in the history of Australian wine, including Lindeman, Wyndham, Penfold, Reynell, and Hardy, were soon joined by an influx of European immigrants—Swiss, Germans, and Silesians, including the de Castellas, de Purys, Henschkes, and Gramps. A strong domestic market was established as well as a fledgling export trade to Britain. Disaster struck Victoria in 1875, when phylloxera arrived and quickly spread across the state. Hundreds of vineyards had to be uprooted and burned. There were also small outbreaks in New South Wales. While Victoria struggled to recover, South Australia and the Barossa Valley prospered.

Hardy Wine Company vineyard, Adelaide Hills, South Australia

 Preceding pages **Wolf Blass vineyard, on the slopes of South Australia's Barossa Valley**

The young wine industry went through a series of booms and busts caused by economic depressions, two world wars, and battles over protective tariffs between the individual states and bounties involving the biggest market, Britain. With rich soils and plenty of sunshine, reds and fortifieds flourished. By the mid-1960s, even though wines bore little resemblance to those of today, the industry could be said to have begun its upswing.

In 1966, 78 percent of Australian wine consumption centered on fortifieds. That was also the year Hunter Valley pioneer Max Lake wrote *Classic Wines of Australia*. He argued that the future lay not in producing "Olympic size pools of sweet fortifieds" but in quality wines made from proven grape varieties. Lake's analysis was perfect. European immigration following World War II had introduced Australian tastes to new wines and foods. Immigrants were regularly buying wine and demanding just the qualities Lake had advocated. Some, like de Bortoli, Miranda, Sergi and Casella, were even getting into wine production themselves.

Modern Trends

By the 1970s, the modern wine industry had been born. It was led by small pioneering producers like Cullen, Cape Mentelle, Pipers Brook, Stonier, and Mount Mary, which explored cooler areas like Margaret River, Tasmania, Mornington Peninsula, and the Yarra Valley. At the top end of the industry, serious rationalization was taking place. Future wine empires like Southcorp Wines, Beringer Blass, and Orlando Wyndham were taking shape through takeovers and mergers.

The industry as we know it began to emerge: stainless steel was widely adopted; new techniques for controlling fermentation temperatures meant that red wine flavors became fruitier; and white wine production became possible even in the hottest regions. Other developments included wine boxes and, more crucially, the advent of easy to recognize varietally labeled Chardonnay and Cabernet Sauvignon. During the 1980s and 90s, the wine industry blossomed until Britain was not the only market taking notice. In quality terms, both its ripe, fruity everyday wines and top-vineyard niche wines have made Australia a global phenomenon.

The Australian wine industry has experienced incredible growth over the past two decades: 20 years ago, there were only 344 wineries; today there are an incredible 1,900, and the number is rising. Vast areas of countryside have been turned over to the vine.

Geographic Indications

Introduced in 1994, the Geographic Indications, or GI, system of labeling Australian wines is based on state and regional boundaries. Wines carrying GI definitions must comply with the 85 percent rule: if a label has a single vintage, region, or variety listed, it must contain 85 percent of the wine stated. The broadest definition, **South Eastern Australia**, takes in all winemaking states except Western Australia. **State** obviously refers to wines produced within a state. **Zone**, part of a state, comprises one or more regions. **Region** is an area that comprises a minimum of five vineyards of at least 12 acres (5 ha) without common ownership and producing at least 500 tons of fruit. A **subregion** has the same requirements, but falls within a region.

Ambitious Plans for Growth

That Australia's winemakers are focused on seducing the world with their wines is beyond question. The stated aims of "Vision 2025," the industry's blueprint for the future, which was published in 1996, are not simply to increase Australia's percentage of the global wine trade, but to make it "the world's most influential and profitable supplier of branded wines," at the same time, pioneering wine as "a universal first choice lifestyle beverage."

Hunter Valley, New South Wales

As recently as 2001, domestic sales of wine were still greater (in terms of volume) than exports. By the end of 2004, however, wine exports of 170 million gallons (650 million liters) had far outstripped the domestic sales of 110 million gallons (420 million liters). The outlook has become much more international. Many of the big Australian winemakers such as Hardy, Beringer Blass, and Southcorp now have strong US connections, while Orlando Wyndham is owned by the French drinks giant Pernod-Ricard. Medium-size winemakers are also consolidating their position in the wine market through vineyard expansion, innovative production techniques, and new marketing strategies. Even the smallest Australian winemaker, producing barely enough bottles to satisfy local demand, now exports wine.

New Frontiers

This growth has led to the exploration of new Australian wine regions like Mount Benson in South Australia (for Shiraz), Orange and Hilltops in New South Wales (for Chardonnay), the Canberra district (for Riesling and Shiraz), and even the cooler, higher altitudes of tropical Queensland (for Chardonnay). A number of areas that in the past would have been considered unsuitable for grape-growing are now under vine.

Viticulture and Vinification

Australian grape-growers and wine producers have always embraced change and employed the latest practices to improve the quality of their wines. The emphasis today is on maximizing the use of water for irrigation and eradicating diseases in the most environmentally responsible way. There is also a growing debate about the reliance on machines for pruning and harvesting versus the benefits of performing these operations by hand.

In the Australian wineries, there is an increasing emphasis on making wines attractive and drinkable early. Wines are being released younger and younger, and practices such as micro-

Wine Regions

Grapes are grown in every state and territory. The key regions, however, are South Australia, Victoria and Tasmania, New South Wales, and Western Australia. There are already almost 70 wine regions within these states, and the number is set to increase.

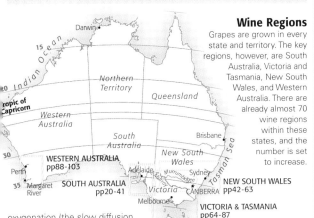

WESTERN AUSTRALIA
pp88-103

SOUTH AUSTRALIA
pp20-41

NEW SOUTH WALES pp42-63

VICTORIA & TASMANIA
pp64-87

oxygenation (the slow diffusion of tiny bubbles into wine during winemaking) can increase color and texture, highlight fruitiness, and mimic the effect of maturation in the barrel.

Choices Facing the Industry

The traditional cross-regional blending practices, which were so commonplace in the past, are still widely employed in the production of lower-priced wines. However, at the top end of the market, the emphasis is now on making a strong regional or single vineyard statement. Winemakers, too, are divided over old versus new: whether they should adopt computer-driven, technologically-smart devices in the winery or use the old-fashioned approach. Concern, and often criticism, over high levels of alcohol and oak in Australian wines are also a source of debate. The challenge for producers is to prove that they are not only capable of making good, popular all-rounders but also of creating world-beating fine wines.

View from modern winery restaurant, Yarra Valley, Victoria

Australian Grape Varieties

Because of the success of Shiraz and Cabernet Sauvignon among the reds and the Chardonnay phenomenon among the whites, the Australian wine industry has become dominated by these three varieties. However, even after more than 200 years of winemaking, Australia is still a relative youngster, and inventive winemakers are busy experimenting with many other varieties.

Red Grape Varieties and Wine Styles

Australia has one of the world's largest plantings of Shiraz (or Syrah) with 96,000 acres (39,000 ha) under vine. South Australia's Barossa Valley and McLaren Vale regions produce the archetypal Australian style, high in sun-ripened flavor and alcohol with generous oak support. In the Hunter Valley (NSW), the grape takes on a more earthy, sun-baked character. Shiraz's nearest rival is Cabernet Sauvignon with 72,900 acres (29,500 ha) planted. It is capable of producing some world-class styles, particularly from Coonawarra and Margaret River, but further expansion of the variety may be limited by the success of its regular blending partner, Merlot (26,700 acres / 10,800 ha). More and more producers are discovering that Merlot can stand by itself, although the style is far from defined as yet. Then there is the

Leading Red Grape Varieties

The three red grapes most widely-grown in Australia are all classic French varieties: Cabernet Sauvignon and Merlot from the Bordeaux region, and Shiraz from the Northern Rhône, though their character changes considerably in the hotter climate.

Syrah/Shiraz
In the New World, France's Syrah grape is usually known as Shiraz. Australia's warmer climate makes for a more powerful, riper style of wine than the Syrah-based wines of southern France, and Shiraz is responsible for some of the country's most profound, desirable wines, particularly in the Barossa and Hunter valleys and McLaren Vale.

Cabernet Sauvignon
World-wide, more quality wines are made from Cabernet Sauvignon than any other red variety. In Australia, as in its native Bordeaux, it may be blended with Merlot and Cabernet Franc, but pure varietal versions are also made, producing wines of intensity and depth. Cabernet Sauvignon is also blended with Shiraz in more everyday wines across Australia.

Merlot
In Australia and other parts of the New World, Merlot is popular both for blending with Cabernet Sauvignon and as a varietal wine. At their best, Australian Merlots have soft tannins and rich, smooth, fruity flavours. Introduced from Europe, Merlot is the dominant variety in the wines of Pomerol and St.-Émilion on Bordeaux's Right Bank.

For more on wine styles See pp136–137

superstar, Pinot Noir. In just over 30 years, Pinot Noir has gone from zero to 10,900 acres (4,400 ha), securing a high public profile along the way thanks to passionate winemakers in southern Victoria and Tasmania.

White Grape Varieties and Wine Styles

When it comes to white wine in Australia, no other grape variety comes close to Chardonnay, with more than 69,200 acres (28,000 ha) under vine. Australian Chardonnay's great strength has traditionally been in sun-ripened, luscious wines to drink early. Today, the emphasis is also on producing top-class Chardonnays with complexity and ageing ability. Australian Semillon (15,400 acres / 6,250 ha) and Riesling (10,500 acres / 4,250 ha) have proven their ability to make top-quality wines, too. Classic unwooded Hunter Valley Semillon is arguably Australia's greatest white wine style; whereas Clare and Eden valleys produce some of the country's best Rieslings.

Grapes for the Future

Australians are looking at other grapes, too. Verdelho and Marsanne provide interesting white alternatives, while the reds Grenache, Mourvèdre (or Mataro), and Petit Verdot are equally at home. Mediterranean varieties Tempranillo, Graciano, Barbera, Sangiovese, Cortese, Primitivo (Zinfandel), and Pinot Gris are yet to be fully explored.

Leading White Grape Varieties

Australia's dependable warmth produces such rich, exuberantly fruity Chardonnays, that, in terms of wine produced, all other white grapes come a distant second. In spite of this, the country is also noted for its distinguished Rieslings and Semillons.

Chardonnay
The world's most popular white variety, Chardonnay generally makes a full-bodied, dry white wine, but its flavor varies from crisp and steely to intense and tropical depending on where it is planted and the winemaking techniques used. Australia makes some of the most intensely flavored examples, full of fuit and often strongly oaked.

Semillon
Semillon makes great dry whites in Australia's Hunter Valley. Made without the use of oak, these wines are light and zesty when young, but then develop delicious toasted aromas with age. Semillon is the main grape in the luscious sweet wines of Sauternes and is paired with Sauvignon Blanc—often fermented in oak—in the dry white wines of Bordeaux.

Riesling
The Riesling grape typically produces a light, fragrant wine with lively acidity, gloriously aromatic flavors, and relatively low alcohol levels, but it can be lusciously sweet and overly fruity. Germany grows more Riesling than any other country, but South Australia has a long tradition of producing fine Rieslings, especially in the Clare and Eden valleys.

Australian Producers: Big and Small

The Australian wine industry has grown at an incredible rate: in 1983, there were 344 commercial wine producers; by 2004 there were 1,899. The majority of Australia's wineries are small, family-owned concerns, but the industry has become dominated by large producers who see themselves as global corporations with global ambitions to match.

THE BIG PLAYERS

Over the past 25 years, the big Australian wine companies have systematically taken over smaller wine producers, acquiring many of the country's most successful brands, turning themselves into stronger, more efficient wine-making machines. Their national and international success is based on producing well-made, fruit-driven wines of mass appeal at highly competitive prices, but they also produce quality wines.

The two largest conglomerates, Southcorp Wines and the Hardy Wine Company, carved out a huge share of the domestic market—about 40 percent of all branded wines sold in Australia. But the takeovers did not stop there. In 2005, Foster's, the Australian beer giant, which already owned the US-Australian Beringer Blass Wine Estates, acquired Southcorp. This gave Foster's 37,000 acres (15,000 ha) of vineyards in Australia, California, New Zealand, Italy, and France, with brands ranging from Lanson Champagne to Penfolds and Lindemans. Australia's five largest companies, including the the two owned by Foster's, are listed below.

Southcorp Wines

Already one of the world's top wine-producing companies when it was bought up by Foster's, Southcorp is a grouping of some of Australia's top producers. It has a strong presence in every winemaking state and makes some of the country's best

Beringer Blass vineyard

Chardonnay and Shiraz. With Foster's distribution, its share of the market can hardly fail to grow.
Producers: *Rosemount Estate* (p58), *Seppelt* (p36), *Seppelt Great Western* (p78), *Wynn's Coonawarra Estate* (p41), *Penfolds* (p37), *Lindemans* (p59), *Devil's Lair, Coldstream Hills* (p83)
Brands: *Koonunga Hill, Grange, St. Henri, Thomas Hyland, Leo Buring, Traditional, Roxburgh, Giant's Creek, Fifth Leg, Hill of Gold, John Riddoch*

Hardy Wine Company

Originally a joining of two major South Australian companies—Hardy Wines and Berri Renmano Ltd.—BRL Hardy merged with US giant Constellation Brands in 2003 to form the world's biggest wine producer. Hardy's strengths are in sparklings, the Banrock Station brand, and McLaren Vale reds.
Producers: *Hardy's* (p40), *Leasingham, Renmano, Houghton* (p98), *Moondah Brook, Banrock Station* (p34), *Reynell, Yarra Burn* (p87) **Brands:** *Omni, Sir James, Arras, Stonehaven, Tintara, Eileen Hardy*

McGuigan Simeon Wines

CEO Brian McGuigan and his family are all involved in this publicly listed company. Fast-

moving and ambitious, it has plans to be the most efficient wine producer in the world.
Producers: *McGuigan (p58), Tempus Two, Miranda*
Brands: *Genus 4, Black Label, River Run, Earth's Portrait, High Country, Vine Vale, Hermitage Road, Cowra Crossing, Howcroft Estate, Pewter Label*

Orlando Wyndham

Orlando Wyndham, owned by French drinks giant Pernod-Ricard, is the face of Australian wine in major markets around the world through its Jacob's Creek brand.
Producers: *Wyndham Estate, Richmond Grove, Poet's Corner (p61), Morris Wines (p82)*
Brands: *Jacob's Creek (p35), Triology, Gramps, Jacaranda Ridge, Centenary Hill, Lawson's, RF Range, St. Hilary, St. Helga, Russet Ridge, Carrington*

Beringer Blass

Foster's—the Australian-based parent of Mildara Blass—bought California's Beringer Wine Estates in 2000 to form Beringer Blass. The company is known in Australia for its great Rieslings and a strong line-up of reds.

VINCENT GASNIER'S
TOP 10
Best of the Big Names

1. **Cape Mentelle** Margaret River *p98*
2. **Penfolds (Foster's)** Barossa Valley & other areas *p37*
3. **Wolf Blass (Foster's)** Barossa Valley & other areas *p36*
4. **Rosemount Estate (Foster's)** Upper Hunter Valley *p58*
5. **Wynn's Coonawarra Estate (Foster's)** Coonawarra *p31*
6. **Yalumba** Barossa Valley *p36*
7. **Hardy Wine Company** McLaren Vale & other areas *p40*
8. **Wyndham Estate (Orlando Wyndham)** Barossa Valley & other areas *p35*
9. **Jacob's Creek (Orlando Wyndham)** many areas *p35*
10. **Lindemans (Foster's)** Upper Hunter Valley & other areas *p59*

Producers: *Mildara Coonawarra, Wolf Blass, Yarra Ridge, Rothbury Estate (p60), St. Hubert's, Saltram, Bailey's of Glenrowan* **Brands:** *Jamiesons Run, Yellowglen, Eaglehawk, Black Opal, Annie's Lane, Robertson's Well, Metala, Mamre Brook, Pepperjack, Greg Norman Estate, Andrew Garrett, Ingoldby, Mt. Ida*

Billboard advertising Orlando Wyndham's ubiquitous Jacob's Creek

Entries for big producers who make wine in many regions of Australia are given under the area of their main winery or original headquarters

SMALL IS BEAUTIFUL

The top 20 large and medium-sized Australian wine producers control about 90 percent of the domestic market. That leaves over 1,800 smaller producers fighting it out for the remaining ten percent of sales of bottled wine. However, what small Australian winemakers lack in size, they more than make up for in other ways. They are the creative heart of the Australian wine industry and the force that has driven it forward over the last 40 years. Almost every wine region in Australia owed its initial development to small makers willing to sink vines into virgin soil to see what succeeded. Some of their vineyards and wineries may since have been swallowed up by one of the large corporations, but a new generation of pioneers has always stepped up to take their place. A few current examples of the remarkable pioneering spirits in the Australian wine industry are given below.

Grosset Wines

Jeffrey Grosset is one of the foremost Riesling makers in Australia. In 2000, he headed a group of his fellow Clare Valley (South Australia) winemakers in bottling Riesling under screwcap, and is now a spokesman for the growing movement away from cork. *See p34.*

Clonakilla

Before it became trendy to blend Shiraz and Viognier in Australia, before Viognier was looked at seriously, and before Canberra was noted for its Riesling, Clonakilla was doing all these things, and doing it with style. Today, Tim Kirk and his father John are rightly viewed as the leading exponents of these wines. *See p62.*

Frankland Estate

Western Australia's rating as a serious maker of Riesling has much to do with the success of Judi Cullam and Barrie Smith's Frankland Estate. They hit the jackpot with Riesling in this far-flung vineyard in the state's southwest. The company now sponsors an annual Riesling tasting and travel award. *See p103.*

Yalumba

Although Yalumba is one of the top 20 wine producers in Australia, it remains an independent family business. Behind its old establishment image lies a company on the move. There is little that does not attract the interest or study of this most

Yalumba's Pewsey Vale vineyard, Eden Valley

Reading an Australian Wine Label

Australia is famous for its no-nonsense varietals, and most wine labels emphasize the grape variety or blend. By law, only 85 percent of the grapes used have to be of the stated variety. Other wines are sold under brand names, which may be blends for the mass market or, as in the example shown below, serious wines by a top winemaker. A Geographical Indication appears on all bottles. This may be a precise wine region such as the Yarra Valley, a state, such as Western Australia, or in the case of many blended wines, an area as vague as Southeast Australia.

Mount Mary Vineyard is the name of the producer. This could be a single estate, as in this case, or a large conglomerate.

Yarra Valley is the Geographical Indication, the region in Victoria where the grapes were grown. There is no obligation by law to give such a precise indication.

MOUNT MARY
VINEYARD
YARRA VALLEY

QUINTET
2002

WINE OF AUSTRALIA
ESTATE BOTTLED AT MOUNT MARY
COLDSTREAM WEST ROAD, LILYDALE, VICTORIA 3140, AUSTRALIA

Alc/Vol 12.5%   PRESERVATIVE 220 ADDED APPROX 7.4 STANDARD DRINKS   750ml

Quintet is the name of the wine. As the name suggests, this wine is a blend of five grape varieties —Cabernet Sauvignon and other Bordeaux varieties. These will be listed on the back label.

2002 indicates vintage— the year in which the grapes were harvested.

Preservative 220 is sulfur dioxide, a permitted additive that helps wine to age well.

Estate Bottled is generally an indication of a serious winemaker.

---

enterprising company. Whether it be Viognier, Riesling, Shiraz, or potentially exciting varieties like Cienna (a cross between Cabernet Sauvignon and the Spanish grape Sumoll), Tempranillo, Petit Verdot, and Marsanne. Many of their exciting new wines are sold under the Vinnovation label. *See p36.*

Giaconda Vineyard

Beechworth-based Rick Kinzbrunner is one of the most influential winemakers in Australia today. His Chardonnay is the standard by which other makers judge their own. He is noted for

his commitment and passion, and there are very few grape varieties he cannot convert into something special. *See p81.*

Pizzini

If the secrets of Italian grape varieties are ever to be fully revealed in Australia, it will be by Fred Pizzini, an Australian-Italian wine grower and maker from the King Valley (Victoria). His quest for authenticity in Nebbiolo, the grape that produces Piedmont's great Barolo, and Sangiovese, the main variety in Chianti, makes for exciting drinking. *See p82.*

SOUTH AUSTRALIA

SOUTH AUSTRALIA

WINE IS BIG BUSINESS *in South Australia. Many of the Australian industry's key players have their headquarters in this hilly state, where flat valley floors rise to beautifully terraced vineyard vistas. A great number of these major wine brands have built their reputation on the high quality of grapes grown in South Australia's key wine areas.*

Adelaide has the site of South Australia's first vineyard, planted by John Barton Hack in 1837. Two years later he planted more vines, this time at a place called Echunga Springs near Mount Barker. But it is South Australia's Barossa Valley that became the beating heart of the early Australian wine industry. In the mid-19th century, this area was settled by industrious immigrants who built impressive wine empires, many of which are still flourishing today. By 1903, Barossa was home to the biggest producer in South Australia, Seppelt *(see p36)*, and the valley was responsible for more than half of the state's total wine crush.

Key

▨ South Australia

However, Barossa has always been rivaled by McLaren Vale. The latter's early history was dominated by three men: John Reynell, Dr. Alexander Kelly, and Thomas Hardy, whose original company Thomas Hardy & Sons grew into the Australian giant Thomas Hardy Wine Company *(see p40)*, largely through trade with Britain. In fact, the British taste for strong, sweet fortified wines and equally strong, heavy reds kept the South Australian wine economy ticking along for almost 100 years.

By the 1950s, artful wine production and a series of smart investments were to cement South Australia's dominance in the nation's wine industry. The introduction of German stainless steel fermentation tanks by Orlando Wines *(see p35)* in 1953 brought a fresh aromatic quality to Barossa whites, notably Riesling. In 1956, Orlando launched Barossa Pearl, Australia's first naturally fermented sparkling wine.

More recently the Adelaide Hills have come to prominence, proving John Barton Hack's inkling all those years ago that this was grape-growing country with great potential. Then there are a number of smaller wine regions such as Piccadilly, the Mount Lofty range, Clare Valley, and Eden Valley, and, much further south, Coonawarra

Old port and sherry casks, Yalumba Winery, South Australia

Preceding pages **Cool-climate vineyards in the Adelaide Hills**

Vineyard in the world-famous Barossa Valley

and Padthaway. Each of these areas has its own distinguishing characteristics of climate and *terroir* that allow connoisseurs to place the wines quite accurately in terms of their provenance.

Today, big names dominate South Australia's winescape, including Southcorp, which is a consolidation of old-time South Australian wine companies such as Penfolds, Leo Buring, and Seppelt. Then there is Beringer Blass, which has a foothold in almost every South Australian wine region (through its Jamiesons Run, Wolf Blass, Saltram, Annie's Lane, Andrew Garrett Wines, Ingoldby, and Maglieri brands). Orlando Wyndham and Hardy Wine Company also still call South Australia home. Over the years, these brands, and the

many copies that followed in their wake, have introduced millions of Australians and—from the 1970s onward—international wine drinkers to South Australian wine. It is from this state that many of Australia's best-known, most celebrated, and expensive wines originate, including Henschke Hill of Grace and Penfolds Grange.

VINCENT GASNIER'S

Blockbuster Australian Reds

1. **Torbreck: Grenache** Barossa Valley *p36*
2. **Henschke: Hill of Grace Shiraz** Eden Valley *p38*
3. **Penfolds: Grange** Barossa Valley *p37*
4. **Brokenwood: Shiraz** Lower Hunter Valley *p58*
5. **Glaetzer: Amon-Ra Shiraz** Barossa Valley *p34*

6. **McGuigan: Cabernet Sauvignon** Lower Hunter Valley *p58*
7. **Tower: Shiraz** Lower Hunter Valley *p60*
8. **Giaconda: Cabernet Sauvignon** Northeast Victoria *p81*
9. **Grant Burge: Cameron Vale Cabernet** Barossa Valley *p35*
10. **Seppelt: St. Peter's Shiraz** Barossa Valley *p36*

Wine Map of South Australia

South Australia's climate zones range from refreshing maritime to warm Mediterranean and hot desert. The hotter regions are naturally suited to ripening red grapes, notably Shiraz—so much so that half of Australia's reds are produced here. Shiraz is the specialty of the Barossa Valley, McLaren Vale, and Clare Valley. Riesling, too, is top-class from Clare, Eden, and Barossa. Coonawarra, on the other hand, is home to some of Australia's finest Cabernet Sauvignon. The Riverland area, Australia's biggest single wine-producing region, can grow anything thanks to irrigation, while the cool Adelaide Hills area is the state's leading Sauvignon Blanc and Pinot Noir producer.

WINE AREAS & MAJOR PRODUCERS

Clare Valley p26
Grosset p34
Jim Barry p34
Wendouree Cellars p34

Riverland p26
Banrock Station p34

Barossa Valley p27
Glaetzer p34
Grant Burge p35
Lehmann p35
Orlando Wyndham p35
Penfolds p37
Seppelt p36
Torbreck p36
Wolf Blass p36
Yalumba p36

Eden Valley p28
Henschke p38
Mountadam p38

Adelaide Hills p29
Petaluma p38
Shaw & Smith p39

McLaren Vale p29
Clarendon Hills p39
Coriole p39
D'Arenberg p40
Hardy Wine Company p40

Langhorne Creek p30
Casa Freschi p40

Mount Benson p30

Padthaway p30

Wrattonbully p31

Coonawarra p31
Bowen p41
Wingara p41
Wynns Coonawarra
  Estate p41

Wallaroo

34°

Maitla

Spencer
Gulf

35°

Gulf St
Vincent

Investigator
Strait

Kingscote

Kangaroo
Island

Penneshaw

36°

View of Barossa Valley vineyards

Regional Information at a Glance

Latitude 33.5–37.5°S.

Altitude 65–1,640 ft (20–500 m).

Topography Expanses of flat terrain in Riverland. Mount Lofty Ranges and adjoining Adelaide Hills provide higher—and thus cooler—growing conditions.

Soil Free-draining limestone and sandy soils, with a constant water table 6.5 ft (2m) below.

Climate Varies greatly, but generally intensely hot and dry. Cooler temperatures near the coast and in the hilly areas.

Temperature January average 64°F (18°C).

Rainfall Annual average 2 in (51.5 mm). In the north the Murray River provides irrigation; in the south vines are irrigated by pipeline from Lake Alexandrina.

Wind Cooling maritime breezes from Gulf St. Vincent provide relief for McLaren Vale, and can penetrate as far inland as Clare Valley.

Viticultural Hazards High winds; spring frosts.

D'Arenberg label, McLaren Vale

Shaw and Smith wines, Adelaide Hills

Wine Areas of South Australia

South Australia

Clare Valley

South Australia's Clare Valley is many things to many drinkers. It is the source of some of Australia's finest and zestiest Riesling *(see p28)*. Its honeyed Semillon has also long been admired, while enthusiasts of hearty red wine have traditionally looked to the valley for succulent but firm Cabernet Sauvignon and gentle, spicy Shiraz. The contrast between the delicacy of its whites and the sheer opulence of its reds could not be greater—a reflection of the variety of subclimates. While the region is warm, there are cooling factors such as southwesterly sea breezes (all the way from Gulf St. Vincent) and the higher altitudes of individual vineyards, with some subregions climbing to 1,800 ft (550 m).

Viticulture in the Clare Valley started early: Mount Horrocks commemorates the first settler, John Horrocks, who planted vines here in 1840. But the golden age of the Clare Valley was in the 1890s, a period that saw the creation of companies such as Wendouree and Stanley, which is now part of the Hardy Wine Company. *red to brown-gray soils with limestone* *Cabernet Sauvignon, Shiraz, Grenache* *Riesling, Chardonnay, Semillon* *red, white, fortified*

Riverland

The "river" in Riverland is the mighty Murray, which stretches right across South Australia and Victoria, bringing life to this hot, arid region. Irrigation from the river sustains 55,350 acres (22,400 ha) of vineyards, which produce an amazing 420,000 tons of grapes annually. Riverland is the biggest vine-growing region of Australia, and every major wine producer in the country sources fruit from this area. The Hardy Wine Company not only has its origins in the area but remains a major presence today, with a 500-strong grower base.

The combination of sun, water, and large-scale viticulture allows economies of scale that big companies appreciate, enabling them to deliver generous fruit-filled wines in the lower price range. In a strong line-up of wines led by ripe, sunny Chardonnay,

Vineyard in the scenic Clare Valley region

  Riverland is sometimes called Murray Valley

Barrels at Yalumba winery, Barossa Valley

a most promising newcomer is spicy Petit Verdot. This red grape, noted for its marked acidity, retains firmness and structure in the Riverland heat. 🌢 *red-brown sandy loam over limestone* 🍇 *Shiraz, Mourvèdre, Grenache, Petit Verdot* 🍇 *Chardonnay, Colombard* 🍷 *red, white, sparkling*

Barossa Valley

The Barossa is the heartland of the Australian wine industry. Many companies that stride the world wine stage started here, including Penfolds, Orlando, Wolf Blass, Henschke, Seppelt, and Yalumba. Most of these wineries were started by a colorful mix of early settlers in the mid-1800s. Some of these were British land-owning gentry, including George Fife Angas, who bought 27,000 acres (11,000 ha) in 1840. He then sold 5,000 acres (2,000 ha) to a number of German and Silesian Lutherans who had come to Australia to escape from religious intolerance in Prussia. Because many settlers came from wine-drinking cultures,

viticulture was naturally adopted as part of general farming in the region. The Lutherans developed vineyards mainly in the valley, while English settlers spread across the Barossa Ranges. By the 1870s, many of these original vineyards were well established, and came to dominate not only winemaking in the region but also Australian winemaking as a whole.

Exports of solid, dry reds and heavy fortifieds to England helped build Barossa Valley into a major winemaking force in the early 20th century. Then, as tastes began to change from red to white wines after World War II, the Barossa changed as well. Refrigeration, the first imported German pressure fermentation tank, and stainless steel tanks helped transform this warm region's white wines into crisp, fruity styles.

There is one grape, however, at which Barossa has always excelled: Shiraz. It achieves levels of power and fruit intensity here that are unmatched elsewhere in Australia, and possibly throughout the world. This grape is the cornerstone of Australia's greatest red, Penfolds Grange, first produced in 1951. 🌢 *brown, loamy sand, gray-brown sand* 🍇 *Shiraz, Cabernet Sauvignon, Grenache* 🍇 *Riesling, Chardonnay, Semillon* 🍷 *red, white, sparkling, fortified*

VINCENT GASNIER'S TOP 10 Great Shiraz Producers in South Australia

1 Glaetzer Barossa Valley *p34*	**6 Penfolds** Barossa Valley *p37*
2 Mitolo McClaren Vale & Barossa Valley *p41*	**7 Yalumba Octavius** Barossa Valley *p36*
3 Geoff Merrill Coonawarra *p41*	**8 Henschke Wines** Eden Valley *p38*
4 Katnook (Wingara) Coonawarra *p41*	**9 Petaluma** Adelaide Hills *p38*
5 Jim Barry: Armagh Clare Valley *p34*	**10 St. Hallett: Old Black** Barossa Valley *p41*

Good recent vintage years in South Australia were 1998, 2000, 2001, 2002, and 2003

Yalumba's Heggies vineyard, Eden Valley

Eden Valley

Also known (confusingly) as the Barossa Ranges, Eden Valley is the cooler, hillier extension of the Barossa Valley. Its history is closely aligned with that of the Barossa, with British and German settlers creating vineyards here between the 1840s and 1860s.

In the cooler, higher southern areas around the towns of Eden Valley and Springton grow some of the best Riesling in Australia. Highly floral and citrussy, Eden Valley Riesling matures quite beautifully over a decade into a toasty, golden wine.

However, it is for Shiraz that Eden Valley is best known. The two producers that have come to dominate the area—Yalumba (see p36) and Henschke (p38)—have found that the relatively warmer northern areas of Angaston, Moculta, and Keyneton bring out the best in the Shiraz grape.

One of Eden Valley's best wines is Henschke's Hill of Grace. It is produced from a 20-acre (8-ha) vineyard of gnarled Shiraz vines planted in a quiet corner of Eden Valley in the 1860s. In around 1960 Cyril Henschke decided to make a special wine from these grapes for the emerging restaurant scene, and nearly half a century later the wine remains one of Australia's great, enduring reds. The vines are dry-grown in sandy and clay loams, sinking their roots deep into ironstone and quartz gravels, giving the wine an extraordinary depth of flavor. Yields are low, so a typical Hill of Grace is intensely concentrated, with blackberry and violet aromas. It also has silky tannins, and contains liquorice, chocolate, and savory flavors highlighted by

The Best Riesling?

Clare and Eden valleys both have a strong history of making quality Riesling. Clare Valley Riesling is resoundingly mineral, with citrus and lime aromas and bracing acidity. That acidity brings an austerity, tautness, and length, and is Clare Riesling's signature trait. In Eden Valley, the grape has generous floral, citrus, and (in some years) even ripe tropical fruit overtones. Elegance is Eden Valley Riesling's main attribute. Most makers keep wines from the two valleys separate, but others, like Wendy Stuckey, chief white winemaker at Wolf Blass (see p36), has proven they go well together, getting the best of both worlds in her top-selling Gold Medal label.

Henschke's Hill of Grace is regarded as one of Australia's icon wines

American oak. Hill of Grace is a wine that also ages very well.

🗺 sandy, clay loams with subsoils of ironstone and quartz gravels 🍇 Shiraz, Cabernet Sauvignon, Pinot Noir 🍷 Riesling, Chardonnay, Semillon 🍾 red, white

Adelaide Hills

Back in the 1970s, Adelaide Hills was filled with fruit orchards. The region had experienced its wine boom 100 years earlier and had moved on due to the public's growing taste for fortified wines, which this cool area could not deliver. But when cool-climate viticulture was explored in the 1970s, the Hills regained attention.

The star name behind the return to winemaking in the area was Brian Croser, former Thomas Hardy winemaker. The 100 percent Adelaide Hills Chardonnays he has made since 1990 rank among the country's best. During the 1990s, cousins Martin Shaw and Michael Hill-Smith (Shaw & Smith) showed the area's potential for creating stunning Sauvignon Blanc. The higher hills—those reaching 2,400 ft (730 m)—also yield a soft, elegant, berry-rich Pinot Noir.

🗺 grey-brown loamy sands, clay loams 🍇 Pinot Noir, Cabernet Sauvignon, Shiraz 🍷 Chardonnay, Sauvignon Blanc, Semillon 🍾 red, white, sparkling

D'Arenberg's winery in McLaren Vale

Super Sauvignon Blanc Territory

The one Australian region capable of giving New Zealand a real run for its money with Sauvignon Blanc is the Adelaide Hills. It is nearly all down to the pioneering influence of true believers such as Martin Shaw and Michael Hill-Smith of Shaw & Smith, who persistently argued its case throughout the 1990s with some great examples. Adelaide Hills Sauvignon Blanc is now a firmly established classic. At its most superb, the style is juicy and succulent, rich in passion fruit and citrus flavors. It is mouth-filling with a zippy acidity and ideally should be drunk within a year of release to be enjoyed at its best.

McLaren Vale

The McLaren Vale made its name producing wine. Walk down the busy main street of McLaren Vale, the town that gives its name to the region, and next to the pub is one of the great wineries of Australia—Tintara—made famous by Thomas Hardy. This Englishman founded the firm that is now known as the Hardy Wine Company (see p40). The region is on the outer suburban fringes of Adelaide, rimmed by Gulf St. Vincent to the west and the Mount Lofty Ranges to the east. The former cools this warm grape-growing region, while the latter offers higher altitudes—up to 1,150 ft (350 m)—which are now being explored for their potential. The main varieties here are sun-drenched Chardonnay and big, bold Shiraz. Well-rounded Cabernets and crisp, medium-bodied Riesling and Sauvignon Blanc can also be found.

🗺 red-brown loamy sands 🍇 Shiraz, Cabernet Sauvignon, Grenache 🍷 Chardonnay, Semillon, Riesling 🍾 red, white, sparkling, dessert, fortified

Kangaroos among the vines, Padthaway

Langhorne Creek

Four of the country's major producers have vineyards here (Southcorp, Orlando Wyndham, Hardy Wine Company, and Beringer Blass). The soft, well-rounded, earthy Cabernet Sauvignon and Shiraz, among other varieties, are used in top-selling wines such as Penfolds Bin 389 Cabernet Shiraz and Wolf Blass Black Label Cabernet Sauvignon, but rarely as stand-alone styles. The grape region's greatest asset—as a blending tool—is also its greatest drawback in terms of better recognition. However, there are some small

local wineries that have developed a Langhorne Creek style. The Potts family of Bleasdale Vineyards have produced wine here—Shiraz and Verdelho—since the 1850s. These varieties and Cabernet are the strength of the region. 🌾 *deep, alluvial sand loams* 🥬 *Cabernet Sauvignon, Shiraz, Merlot* 🍇 *Chardonnay, Verdelho, Riesling* 🍷 *red, white*

Mount Benson

This fast-developing region came to prominence after the Rhône winemaker M. Chapoutier created a vineyard in 1998, indicating a future for a Rhône-style Australian Shiraz. The big Australian wine companies buy grapes here. 🌾 *sandy clay to clay loams over limestone and siliceous sands* 🥬 *Shiraz, Cabernet Sauvignon, Merlot* 🍇 *Chardonnay, Sauvignon Blanc, Semillon* 🍷 *red, white*

Padthaway

Attracting the attention of wine firms in the 1960s as a cheaper source of grapes than nearby Coonawarra, the Padthaway region has taken time to achieve recognition in its own right. The creation of Hardy's

Magnificent Celebration Wines

1. **Yalumba: Cabernet Sauvignon Reserve** (red) Barossa Valley *p36*
2. **Henschke: Hill of Grace Shiraz** (red) Eden Valley *p38*
3. **Torbreck: Grenache** (red) Barossa Valley *p36*
4. **Penfolds: Grange** (red) Barossa Valley *p37*
5. **Giaconda: Shiraz** (red) Northeast Victoria *p81*
6. **Seppelt: Chardonnay** (white) Barossa Valley *p36*
7. **Penfolds: Yattarna Chardonnay** (white) Adelaide Hills *p37*
8. **Leeuwin Estate: Art Series Chardonnay** (white) Margaret River *p100*
9. **Grosset: Chardonnay** (white) Clare Valley *p34*
10. **Brokenwood: Shiraz** (red) Hunter Valley *p58*

Stonehaven Winery in the 1990s finally brought it the attention it deserves. 🏞 *loamy sand soils with isolated limestone* 🍇 *Shiraz, Cabernet Sauvignon, Merlot, Pinot Noir* 🍇 *Riesling, Chardonnay, Semillon* 🍷 *red, white*

Wrattonbully

Bordering Coonawarra, the Wrattonbully area has traditionally grown elegant Shiraz and Cabernet Sauvignon, which have sometimes been bottled as Coonawarra. Wrattonbully is now a completely separate area under the Geographical Indications Process *(see p11).* 🏞 *sandy clay to clay loams over limestone* 🍇 *Cabernet Sauvignon, Shiraz, Merlot* 🍇 *Chardonnay, Sauvignon Blanc, Semillon* 🍷 *red, white*

Coonawarra

The color of Coonawarra is red: the wines are mainly red and the soil is a dazzling red-brick hue. This soil, known as *terra rossa*, is behind Coonawarra's claim to be Australia's greatest red wine region. The *terra rossa* strip is 9 miles (15 km) long and varies in width from about 650 ft (200 m)

The Coonawarra Boundary Dispute

This boundary dispute began in 1984, focusing on a "cigar-shaped" area of rich, red soils known as *terra rossa.* As it became planted out, makers moved into adjoining soils where pockets of *terra rossa* could be found. Over time, these producers considered their wines to be comparable to those from the "cigar". This was the basis for the great boundary battle. A 1999 court decision saw 46 producers fall outside the boundary. They appealed, and in 2001 a tribunal allowed 24 (including Petaluma) back inside. A further appeal in 2002 saw the Federal Court allow another five growers (including Beringer Blass) back in.

to 1 mile (1.5 km). Beneath a thin layer of well-drained red soil lies soft limestone that holds water reserves, which the vines exploit. The region is classified as cool (hard to believe in summer), with a long ripening period. This gives Cabernet Sauvignon a firm tannic quality, making it ideal for ageing. The style is firm, concentrated, and the most Bordeaux-like of all Australian Cabernet— often with a touch of mint. An array of producers excel with the Cabernet here, including Wynn's, Bowen, Hollick, Lindemans, Jamiesons Run, Majella, Brand's, and Katnook. Hard as it is for other varieties to make any kind of significant showing here, the region does manage to produce a rather underrated earthy Shiraz and floral Riesling. 🏞 *red soil and black clays over limestone* 🍇 *Cabernet Sauvignon, Shiraz, Pinot Noir* 🍇 *Chardonnay, Riesling, Sauvignon Blanc* 🍷 *red, white*

The famous *terra rossa* (red earth) of Coonawarra

The southeastern corner of South Australia is called the Limestone Coast

A Penfolds vineyard in the Clare Valley

Major Producers in South Australia

Grosset Wines
Clare Valley

Jeffrey Grosset's approach to winemaking is all about attention to detail. And his skill for fine-tuning is never more evident than when he's artfully blending batches of Riesling. His Polish Hill Riesling (tight and minerally in style) and Watervale Riesling (with its citrus and aromatic character) are at the top of the Australian tree for this famous German grape. Grosset has also ventured into new winemaking territory, with a Piccadilly Chardonnay using grapes from the Adelaide Hills and Gaia, a complex Clare Valley Cabernet Sauvignon blend. ✪ *Stanley St., Auburn • 08 8849 2175 • www.grosset. com.au ❑ ▣ red, white ★ Polish Hill Riesling, Watervale Riesling, Gaia*

Jim Barry Wines
Clare Valley

Though Jim Barry died in 2003, his descendants have kept the name. The best-known product is the powerful Armagh Shiraz, from the vineyard of the same name, which was planted by Jim himself in 1968. It is a shame that demand for this explosive wine has made it expensive. Fortunately, stepping in to fill the breach is the McRae Wood Shiraz—strong in blackberry fruits with a touch of mintiness. The fragrant Jim Barry Watervale Riesling is another fantastic bargain. ✪ *Craigs Hill Rd., Clare • 08 8842 2261 ❑ ▣ red, white ★ Watervale Riesling, The Armagh Shiraz, McRae Wood Shiraz*

Wendouree Cellars
Clare Valley

Tony Brady took over this 19th-century vineyard in the 1970s and has built up a reputation for sublime wines. A rarity in today's fast-moving Australian wine industry, Brady seeks no publicity, yet his wines sell out regardless. He fashions powerful Shiraz and complex Cabernet Sauvignon (as well as assorted blends) around viselike tannic structures that require time in the cellar to mature. ✪ *Wendouree Rd., Clare • 08 8842 2896 ❑ ▣ red, fortified ★ Shiraz, Cabernet Sauvignon, Cabernet Sauvignon-Malbec*

Banrock Station
Riverland

A wine and wetland center by the Murray River, Banrock Station is an initiative of the Hardy Wine Company *(see p40)*. The reds include a rich and plummy Shiraz, chocolatey Merlot, and a strong, blackberry-tinged Petit Verdot. Best of all is a lively sparkling Shiraz that belies its moderate price with great depth. ✪ *Holmes Rd., Kingston on Murray • 08 8583 0299 • www.banrockstation.com.au ❑ ▣ red, white, sparkling ★ Sparkling Shiraz, Cave Cliff Merlot, Ball Island Shiraz*

Glaetzer
Barossa Valley

Glaetzer's main business is high-volume contract winemaking: in 2005 it produced 1,300 different wines for other companies. However, it also releases under its own label, specializing in Barossa

Valley reds from old vines. The astonishing premium Shiraz, Amon-Ra, has firm structure with ripe and supple tannins giving support to blackcurrant and nutmeg flavors. *Barossa Valley Way, Tanunda • 08 8563 0288 • www.glaetzer. com* 🔲 🍷 *red* ★ *Amon-Ra, Godolphin Shiraz Cabernet, Bishop Shiraz*

Grant Burge Wines
Barossa Valley
Burge's insistence on promoting a uniquely Barossan product explains his status as the largest private holder of the area's vineyards. Each year, his company processes 6,500 tons of local fruit (red wines are produced at the Illaparra Winery, whites at the Barossa Vines Winery), and quantity is matched by quality. The Mesach Shiraz and Cameron Vale Cabernet are some of Australia's best red wines. The fact that 50 per cent of his vineyards are dedicated to young vines bodes well for the results of Burge's penchant for innovation. *Jacobs Creek, Tanunda • 08 8563 3700 • www.grantburgewines.com.au* 🔲 🍷 *red, white, sparkling, fortified* ★ *Mesach Shiraz, Cameron Vale Cabernet, Chardonnay NV, 20 Year Old Tawny Port*

Orlando Wyndham
Barossa Valley & other areas
The creek that has flooded the world—Jacob's Creek—began life in 1976 in the Barossa Valley. The brand was revolutionary: a fruit-driven, early drinking, good-value Shiraz-Cabernet Sauvignon. In 1990, the producer of Jacob's Creek, Orlando Wines, joined up with Wyndham Estate in New South Wales to form Orlando Wyndham, Australia's largest wine and spirits group, which, in turn, is a subsidiary of drinks giant Pernod Ricard. As well as Jacob's Creek, the most notable labels under the

Orlando Wines umbrella are the Steingarten and St. Helga Rieslings, the tropical St. Hilary Chardonnay, the Jacaranda Ridge and St. Hugo Cabernet Sauvignons, and the warm single-vineyard Centenary Hill Shiraz. The Wyndham Estate arm includes the 1828 and Bin ranges. The group also owns Richmond Grove in Barossa and Poet's Corner *(see p61)* in Mudgee. *www. orlandowines.com, www.wyndhamestate. com • Jacob's Creek Visitor Centre: Rowland Flat, 08 8521 3000, www. jacobscreek.com* 🔲 🍷 *red, white, sparkling, dessert, fortified* ★ *Jacob's Creek, Jacaranda Ridge, Steingarten, Wyndham Estate*

Penfolds
Barossa Valley
See p37.

Peter Lehmann Wines
Barossa Valley
Big, warm, hospitable Peter Lehmann is a true Barossa wine legend, although son Doug and the winemakers Leonie Lange and Andrew Wigan now run the business. The company specializes in traditional Barossa styles, and they don't come any bigger than Peter Lehmann Shiraz, with its full fruit flavors and oak punch. Peter Lehmann's other Shiraz wines include the seductive, sparkling Black Queen and the long-lived Stonewell. The most heavenly flavors, however, appear in the gorgeous Eight Songs Shiraz. The Vintage "port" again uses predominantly Shiraz. By contrast, Lehmann's nuanced, aromatic Riesling and lemony Sémillon show great subtlety. *Off Para Rd., Tanunda • 08 8563 2500 • www.peterlehmannwines.com.au* 🔲 🍷 *red, white, sparkling, dessert, fortified* ★ *Black Queen Sparkling Shiraz, Blue Eden Riesling, Eight Songs Shiraz*

Orlando Wyndham produces more than 5 million cases of Jacob's Creek each year, which it exports to over 60 countries

Seppelt Winery
Barossa Valley

Founded by Joseph Seppelt in 1867, a century later this winery was producing sparkling, still, and fortified wines across three states. The Seppelt family maintained control of their empire until 1984, when they merged with South Australia Brewing. Now part of Southcorp *(see p16)*, Seppelt is a showpiece winery producing distinguished fortifieds. Top billing is shared by a super-tangy Fino, an elegant, nutty Tawny, and a dry, complex Amontillado. The winery has a treasure-trove of old fortified blending material, enabling it to release a 100-year-old tawny "port" each year at thousands of Australian dollars per bottle. ◈ *Seppeltsfield via Nuriootpa • 08 8568 6217 • www.seppelt. com.au* ❑ 🖼 *red, white, sparkling, fortified* ★ *Show Fino DP 117, Show Amontillado DP 116, Show Tawny DP 90*

Wolf Blass Winery
Barossa Valley

German-born Wolf Blass is a brash but endearing self-promoter. One of his renowned quotes is: "My wines make weak men strong and strong women weak". Moving to Australia in 1961, Blass brought a touch of chutzpah to winemaking, and it has rewarded him with a hugely successful business built around an old army shed-cum-winery at Nuriootpa in the Barossa. Today, that same shed site houses an AUS$30 million superwinery – an integral part of the Beringer Blass empire. The core of Wolf Blass wines is made up of a highly approachable range of Rieslings, and strong, oak-driven Shiraz and Cabernet Sauvignon. ◈ *97 Sturt Hwy, Nuriootpa • 08 8568 7311 • www. wolfblass.com.au* ❑ 🖼 *red, white, sparkling, dessert, fortified* ★ *Platinum Label: Barossa Cabernet Sauvignon, Barossa Shiraz, Gold Label Riesling*

Torbreck Vintners
Barossa Valley

David Powell's accountancy background might explain the business sense that underlies his artful production process. He hand-crafts wines using grapes from old-vine Barossa vineyards to create small-yield products whose excellence guarantees demand. Torbreck's output is derived principally from Shiraz, Grenache, and Mataro, the first two of which enable Powell to pay homage to wines from the Rhône Valley in France. The flagship wine, Runrig, is a high-quality, high-priced red that contains fruit from dry-farmed Shiraz vineyards, blended with a little Viognier. ◈ *Roennfeldt Rd., Tanunda • 08 8562 4155 • www.torbreck. com* ❑ 🖼 *red, white* ★ *Runrig, Les Amis Grenache, The Steading, Woodcutters*

Yalumba
Barossa Valley, Eden Valley

Samuel Smith, an Englishman, founded Yalumba (Aboriginal for "all the country around") in 1849. Today, his great-great-grandson Robert heads the innovative company, which has sustained incredible growth through the family purse alone. With its warm and friendly style, Barossa Shiraz is the headliner red. The Eden Valley is home to Yalumba's Pewsey Vale and Heggies vineyards, which produce strong Riesling and Viognier respectively. The Pewsey Vale Riesling has delicate, citrussy notes, while the Viognier comes in many guises, from the drink-now Heggies Vineyard Viognier to the opulent, ginger-spiced Virgilius. ◈ *Eden Valley Rd., Angaston • 08 8561 3200 • www.yalumba.com* ❑ 🖼 *red, white, sparkling, dessert, fortified* ★ *Barossa Shiraz-Viognier, The Virgilius Viognier, Pewsey Vale*

The Penfolds Success Story

No other wine company in the world can match Penfolds for the sheer quality and variety of wines across all price categories—from the AUS$10 Rawson's Retreat to the AUS$400 bottle of Grange. As part of Southcorp, Australia's biggest winemaker, Penfolds has access to an unequaled range of vineyard and winemaking resources, including thousands of hectares of vines across all states – though South Australia remains its base.

Dr. Christopher Rawson Penfold arrived at Magill near Adelaide in 1844 and planted vines, mostly Grenache. Palomino, Muscat, and Frontignac were also grown around the Penfold family's cottage, "The Grange". Dr. Penfold believed in the medicinal value of wine and used it as a tonic for his patients. After his death, generations of the family continued his work in the vineyard, cementing a Penfolds winemaking tradition. In 1911, a winery was built in the Barossa Valley, which became Penfolds HQ.

Winemakers
Since Max Schubert—the creator of the Grange wine range—was at the helm in the 1950s, there have been just four chief winemakers. The latest, Peter Gago *(left)*, is keenly aware that the market expects Penfolds' traditions to be maintained to ensure a continuity of style.

Contact Information

Tanunda Rd, Nuriootpa
• 08 8301 5569 • www. penfolds.com.au ☐

Wine Information

🟥 red, white, fortified
★ Penfolds Grange, Bin 707 Cabernet Sauvignon, Yattarna Chardonnay, Bin 389 Cabernet Sauvignon-Shiraz

Penfolds Wine
While multiregional blending has brought consistency, Penfolds wines are rooted in the Barossa Valley, with a style of ripe, rich, sweet fruit, often oak influenced, with rounded tannins. At the heart of the brand is a range of individual styles: a peppery Bin 128 Shiraz, a ripe, full-flavoured Bin 389 Cabernet-Shiraz, and—most elegant of all—a Bin 707 Cabernet Sauvignon.

South Australia–Producers

Dr. Penfold's first vineyard at Magill, Adelaide, photographed here in 1958

 In the 1920s, half of all Australian wines had a Penfolds label

Henschke Wines
Eden Valley

Stephen and Prue Henschke make a formidable team: Stephen is a winemaker who treasures the 19th-century vineyard he has inherited from the Henschke generations before him; and Prue, his wife, is a viticulturist with an excellent understanding of the winemaking process. When they took over here in 1980, they set out to make their own mark by improving the trellising system in the vineyards and opening up the vines to sunlight. The fruit intensity achieved since then, coupled with the complexity that comes from low-yielding old vines, has resulted in red wines of great finesse. The richly concentrated Hill of Grace flagship wine *(see p28)*, developed by Stephen's father, Cyril, is followed by the fleshy Mount Edelstone Shiraz and the elegant Cyril Henschke Cabernet Sauvignon.
Henschke Rd, Keyneton • 08 8564 8223 • www.henschke.com.au □ 🍷 *red, white ★ Hill of Grace Shiraz, Mount Edelstone Shiraz, Cyril Henschke Cabernet Sauvignon*

Mountadam Vineyards
Eden Valley

Founded in 1972 by the late David Wynn and his son, Adam, Mountadam was always going to be different. David was the man responsible for the development of the first commercial wine barrel in Australia, and was also behind Wynn's Coonawarra Estate. He and his son were among the first to promote unwooded Chardonnay in Australia, as well as an unwooded Shiraz. In contrast, the premium Mountadam range is positively baroque in opulence, led by an amazingly rich traditional method sparkling and buttery Chardonnay. The leading red, simply called The Red, is a supple blend of Merlot and Cabernet Sauvignon. Organically grown wines are championed here under the Eden Ridge label. In 2000, Adam accepted a takeover bid by Cape Mentelle *(see p98)*, and since then the business has shown no loss of quality. 🍷 *High Eden Rd., Eden Valley • 08 85 64 1900 • www.mountadam.com □* 🍷 *red, white, sparkling, dessert ★ Eden Valley Riesling, Chardonnay, The Red*

Petaluma Limited
Adelaide Hills & other areas

In 1976, the charismatic Brian Croser—formerly a winemaker at Hardy's *(see p40)*—decided to go it alone and set up Petaluma, aspiring to create the finest wines from prime locations in South Australia. He sources pristine Riesling from Clare Valley and elegant Cabernet Sauvignon from Coonawarra, which is used in a red blend named after the area. When Croser made his HQ at Bridgewater in the then little-known Adelaide Hills, he planted Chardonnay in the nearby Piccadilly Valley. Within a decade, these three varieties became Australian benchmarks, carrying the Croser stamp of purity and elegance, and reflecting what to many Australian drinkers was a new concept: *terroir*—or, as Croser says, "distinguished vineyard sites." Since 2000 Croser has been working on some new

Label from Petaluma

Brian Croser at Petaluma is one of Australia's most influential winemakers

styles, including a vibrant Shiraz and an apricot-rich Viognier. ◈ *Spring Gully Rd., Piccadilly • 08 8339 4122 • www.petalumalimited.com* ☐ ▣ *red, white, sparkling, dessert* ★ *Hanlin Hill Riesling, Tiers Chardonnay, Coonawarra*

Shaw & Smith
Adelaide Hills
Michael Hill-Smith was Australia's first Master of Wine, and his cousin Martin Shaw was one of Australia's first flying winemakers. They came together in 1989 to create Shaw & Smith, firing winelovers' imaginations

Michael Hill-Smith and Martin Shaw of Shaw & Smith

with a bright and tropical Sauvignon Blanc. The crusading duo then went on to cement the reputation of the Adelaide Hills as a serious Chardonnay region—first with an appley, unwooded version and then with a wooded style that carries overtones of stone fruits. In 2001, a noticeably lean and citrous Chardonnay, M3 Vineyard, came out. ◈ *Jones Rd., Balhannah • 08 8398 0500 • www.shawandsmith. com* ☐ ▣ *red, white* ★ *Sauvignon Blanc, M3 Vineyard Chardonnay, Merlot*

Clarendon Hills
McLaren Vale
The wines of Clarendon Hills are among the biggest and most concentrated reds Australia can offer. These goliaths—mostly Shiraz, Cabernet Sauvignon, and Grenache—are the creation of media-shy winemaker Roman Bratasiuk. He sources old-vine, low-yielding grapes from the subregions of McLaren Vale. This has spawned a growing range headed by the super-rich Astralis Shiraz, which now enjoys cult status with collectors. As it is out of most people's price range there

are other reds filling the gap, notably the lovely Liandra Shiraz and the rustic Roma's Vineyard Old Vine Grenache. ◈ *363 The Parade, Kensington Park • 08 8364 1484 • www. clarendonhills.com.au* ☐ *by appt* ▣ *red, white* ★ *Astralis Shiraz, Liandra Shiraz, Roma's Vineyard Old Vine Grenache*

Coriole
McLaren Vale
This is a little slice of Tuscany in Australia, with terraced vineyards, olive trees, and fine Sangiovese wines. Owners Mark and Paul Lloyd were among the first to plant Sangiovese in Australia (in the 1980s). They embrace the wine both as a stand-alone style, rich in savory cherry fruit, and as an earthy blending tool. The red ironstone here weaves a subtle mineral quality into red wines, which are balanced with gentle tannins. Top of the tree is the Lloyd Reserve Shiraz, but Coriole also does well with the easy-drinking white Lalla Rookh Semillon. ◈ *Chaffeys Rd., McLaren Vale • 08 8323 8305 • www.coriole.com* ☐ ▣ *red, white* ★ *Lalla Rookh Semillon, Sangiovese-Shiraz, Lloyd Reserve Shiraz*

South Australia–Producers

Chardonnay grapes ripening at a vineyard in the McLaren Vale

The purchase of Banrock Station *(see p34)* fueled spectacular growth in the wine box and quaffing markets. Old-time brands Houghton, Leasingham, and Château Reynella were spruced up, and BRL Hardy became the consummate Australian wine success story.

Over the past decade, there has been a huge surge in the quality of Hardy's sparkling wines under winemaker Ed Carr. The good-value Omni range segues into the mid-range Sir James—with its fantastic appley-citrus vintage and a spicy sparkling Shiraz—while the top-line Arras makes use of traditional Champagne grapes, Pinot Noir, and Chardonnay. The Eileen Hardy brand name represents the flagship white (a complex Chardonnay) and red (a hearty McLaren Vale Shiraz). ⊗ *Reynell Rd, Reynella* • *08 8340 2568* • *www.hardywines.cam.au* ☐ ☒ *red, white, sparkling, dessert, fortified* ★ *Arras Vintage Sparkling, Eileen Hardy: Chardonnay, Shiraz*

D'Arenberg
McLaren Vale
This estate has released many memorable reds (and names to match) since the brand was revamped in the 1990s, including Dead Arm Shiraz and The Laughing Magpie Shiraz-Viognier. The bevy of whites include a mineral-rich Olive Grove Chardonnay and The Hermit Crab Marsanne-Viognier— the latter notable for honeysuckle undertones. ⊗ *Osborn Rd, McLaren Vale* • *08 8323 8206* • *www.darenberg. com.au* ☐ ☒ *red, white, sparkling, dessert, fortified* ★ *The Hermit Crab, Dead Arm, Ironstone Pressings*

Hardy Wine Company
McLaren Vale & other areas
In 2003 BRL Hardy signed a multi-billion-dollar merger with US wine company Constellation Brands to form the biggest wine business in the world. This was a far cry from 1992, when one of Australia's great family-run wine empires, Thomas Hardy & Sons, was in serious financial trouble and taken over by Berri Renmano. The road back to the top started with the acquisition of some prestigious estates in desirable areas, such as Yarra Burn (Yarra Valley), Brookland Valley (Margaret River), and Nobilo in New Zealand *(see p119)*.

Casa Freschi
Langhorne Creek
David Freschi worked in Italy, California, and New Zealand, before returning to Langhorne Creek in 1998 to work on his parents' vineyard. His first release wines were a huge success. La Signora ("the lady") is an unusual blend of Cabernet Sauvignon, Shiraz, Nebbiolo, and Malbec with chocolate and licorice flavors. Profondo Shiraz-Cabernet is a velvety wine that lives up to its name. ⊗ *30 Jackson Ave, Strathalbyn* • *08 8536 4569* • *www.casafreschi. com. au* ◒ ☒ *red* ★ *La Signora, Profondo*

The Hardy Wine Company accounts for 25 percent of the domestic Australian market and exports to more than 60 countries

Bowen Estate
Coonawarra

Doug Bowen is regarded as the champion of Shiraz in Cabernet-crazy Coonawarra. There are some mighty tannins and alcohol at work in a young Bowen Shiraz that need at least five years to achieve their potential. His 1998 Ampelon Shiraz is from a low-yielding vineyard, and the resulting flavors are deeply concentrated. Bowen says his Cabernet Sauvignon pretty much makes itself, but this cedary, blackberry wine is more generous than many. ✆ *Riddoch Highway, Coonawarra* • *08 8737 2229* ▢ 🖾 *red, white, sparkling* ★ *Ampelon Shiraz, Shiraz, Cabernet Sauvignon*

Wingara Wine Group
Coonawarra

The high-quality, limited-release products of Katnook Estate are the most prominent names in Wingara's portfolio. Katnook Founder's Block is a range of informal drinking wines; Riddoch flies the flag for Coonawarra fruit, an honor that has now been extended to the Faldo brand, in association with the golfer Nick Faldo. ✆ *Highway, Coonawarra* • *08 8737 2394* • *www.wingara.com.au* ▢ 🖾 *red, white* ★ *Katnook Estate Odyssey Cabernet Sauvignon, Katnook Estate Merlot 2000*

Wynns Coonawarra Estate Winery
Coonawarra

David Wynn has steered away from the Bordeaux style aspired to by many Coonawarra producers and instead created a laid-back Australian Cabernet. Known widely as Wynns Black Label, it is bold, fruity, and warm, with a hint of cedary oak. Move up a notch to the John Riddoch Cabernet and everything, especially the oak, is amplified. The standard, earthy Wynns Shiraz is everyday fare, but the Michael Shiraz demands at least 10 years to quieten down those oak tannins. Winemaker Sue Hodder turns out a quality, lemony Riesling too. ✆ *Memorial Dr, Coonawarra* • *08 8736 2225* • *www.wynns.com.au* ▢ 🖾 *red, white* ★ *Riesling, John Riddoch Cabernet Sauvignon, Michael Shiraz*

Other Producers in South Australia

Charles Melton Wines *(Barossa Valley)* Krondorf Rd, Tanunda • 08 8563 3606 • www.charlesmeltonwines.com.au

Heggies *(Barossa Valley)* Eden Valley Rd, Angaston • 08 8561 3200 • www.heggiesvineyard.com

Hollick Winery *(Coonawarra)* 08 8737 2318 • www.hollick.com

Geoff Merrill *(Adelaide Hills)* Pimpala Rd, Woodcroft • 08 8381 6877 • www.geoffmerrillwines.com

Kilikanoon Wines *(Clare Valley)* Penna Lane, Penwortham • 08 8843 4377 • www.kilikanoon.com.au

Leo Buring *(Eden & Clare valleys)* Owned by Foster's • www.fosters.com.au

Majella Wines *(Coonawarra)* 08 8736 3055 • www.majellawines.com.au

Mitolo *(McLaren Vale and Barossa Valley)* Angel Vale Rd, Angel • 08 8282 9012 • www.mitolowines.com.au

Nepenthe Wines *(Adelaide Hills)* Vickers Rd, Lenswood • 08 8431 7588 • www.nepenthe.com.au

Penley Estate *(Coonawarra)* McLeans Rd • 08 8736 3211 • www.penley.com.au

Stafford Ridge *(Adelaide Hills)* Stafford Rd, Lenswood • 08 8272 2105

St Hallett *(Barossa Valley)* St Hallett's Rd, Tanunda • 08 8563 7000 • www.sthallett.com.au

Taylors *(Clare Valley)* Taylors Rd, Auburn 08 8849 1111 • www.taylors.com.au

Turkey Flat *(Barossa Valley)* Bethany Rd, Tanunda • 08 8563 2851 • www.turkeyflat.com.au

NEW SOUTH WALES

NEW SOUTH WALES

A STATE OF EXTREMES, NEW SOUTH WALES *is no Garden of Eden for vines. From the tropical north to the snow-capped Alps in the south, winemakers here have succeeded against the odds, yet many of the great names of the Australian wine industry now call New South Wales home.*

The Australian wine industry can be said to have begun in New South Wales (NSW) when the first governor, Arthur Phillip, and the early settlers planted vines. The results of these first trial plantings were disappointing, and the industry did not really begin to prosper until two determined 19th-century pioneers—George Wyndham in the late 1820s and Dr. Henry Lindeman *(see p59)* in the 1840s—discovered an area with soil and a climate conducive to growing grapes for wine: the Lower Hunter Valley, about 103 mi (165 km) north of Sydney. By 1850, vineyards planted there had clearly demonstrated the suitability of grapes like Shiraz and Semillon to the region.

The Lower Hunter Valley has kept its reputation as one of the country's top wine regions and, when Australian wine underwent its great renaissance in the 1960s and 1970s, the area experienced a colonial-style "gold rush" to open up new land for wine production. Vineyards were also established in the previously unexploited Upper Hunter Valley.

A little further inland, on the other side of the Great Dividing Range, the Mudgee region had vines growing by 1858, but it was the expansion of well-known producer Orlando Wyndham's Hunter facilities to Mudgee in

Key

Wine areas of
New South Wales

1997 that really helped promote the region. Pride in Mudgee wines, led by fine Shiraz, Cabernet Sauvignon, and Chardonnay, has been growing ever since.

Irrigating the Interior

The Hunter Valley may be the source of the state's finest wines, but its output is relatively small. More than half the wine produced in New South Wales today is grown in the vast Riverina district. This amounts to 15 percent of Australia's total national production. In the late 19th century, this hot, dry region was a sparsely populated sheep-grazing district. An ambitious plan was conceived to build an irrigation canal and open up the land for agriculture. The Murrumbigee was dammed, and in 1912 the canal delivered water to the area. Among the first farmers to move in was J.J. McWilliam, founder of the McWilliam's family business *(see p59)*, who planted vines there in 1913. The first vintage was in 1916, the year the township of Griffith was proclaimed, named after the New South Wales Minister for Public Works, who had overseen the scheme.

After World War I, farm holdings expanded rapidly with the help of government settlement schemes for returning soldiers. New crops were tried, including rice, which

Preceding pages **View of the Hunter Valley, the key wine-producing region of New South Wales**

Grape picking at Tyrrell's in the Hunter Valley

still plays an important part in the region's economy. The wine industry expanded, too: Penfolds was established here in 1921, followed by De Bortoli in 1928. Riverina gained a reputation for cheapness, supplying huge quantities for the boxed wine market of the 1970s and 80s, but today produces ripe, clean fruit for more palatable drinking.

Recent Developments
Since the 1970s, the rise of cool-climate viticulture has seen the exploration of many other regions of New South Wales, such as

Hilltops, Orange, and the enclave of Canberra (Australian Capital Territory). These now produce some of the region's most exciting wines with firmer tannin structures, more pronounced acidity, and less of the usual sun-baked, fruity character.

Today, New South Wales is the country's third largest wine state. It boasts 92,400 acres (37,400 ha) of vines grown by producers such as Lindemans, Wyndham, Tyrrell's, and McWilliam's—a feat that would not have been thought possible two decades, never mind two centuries, ago.

VINCENT GASNIER'S
TOP 10 Best-Kept Secrets in Australian Wine

1. **Glaetzer: Bishop Shiraz**
   (red) Barossa Valley *p34*
2. **Frankland: Merlot**
   (red) Great Southern *p103*
3. **Allandale: Cabernet Sauvignon**
   (red) Lower Hunter Valley *p56*
4. **Voyage Estate: Chardonnay**
   (white) Margaret River *p101*
5. **Cullen: Cabernet Sauvignon-Merlot**
   (red) Margaret River *p99*
6. **Tahbilk: Marsanne**
   (white) Goulburn Valley *p80*
7. **Brokenwood: Shiraz**
   (red) Lower Hunter Valley *p58*
8. **Clonakilla: Shiraz-Viognier**
   (red) Canberra District *p62*
9. **Moss Wood: Cabernet Sauvignon Blend** (red) Margaret River *p100*
10. **Henschke: Semillon**
    (white) Eden Valley *p38*

Wine Map of New South Wales

New South Wales boasts Australia's number one wine destination: the Hunter Valley. The Lower Hunter produces two world-class varietal wines—age-worthy Semillon and earthy Shiraz. The Upper Hunter and Mudgee are associated with rich Chardonnay, while the newly emerging Orange and Hilltops areas, further south, are delivering more minerally examples of Chardonnay, as well as fleshy Shiraz. The larger Riverina area, known for its bulk production, also makes a generous Shiraz, and Semillon excels here, too. Toward the coast, the emerging Canberra district is delivering floral Rieslings, peppery Shiraz, and excellent Pinot Noir.

WINE AREAS & MAJOR PRODUCERS

Water pump surrounded by vineyards, Mudgee

Winemaker testing wine at De Bortoli, Riverina

Regional Information at a Glance

Latitude 32–36.5°S.

Altitude 33–2,950 ft (10–900 m).

Topography The Hunter Valley, the Canberra District, and Mudgee all feature undulating hills and flood plains, while the Orange, Cowra, Hilltops, and Tumbarumba areas are mountainous, so vineyards are at much higher altitudes. The Murrumbidgee River provides a lifeline in the hot inland growing region of Riverina.

Soil Mostly red clay or sand, with rich volcanic soil in the Orange region.

Climate The Lower Hunter is warm and humid; the Upper Hunter is drier. Moderate climate (Mudgee); cool in the foothills of Mount Canobolas (Orange); warm and dry (Cowra). Riverina is hot and dry—irrigation here is vital, whereas Canberra alternates between warm and cool.

Temperature January average is 81°F (27°C).

Rainfall Annual average 25–30 in (630–750 mm).

Viticultural Hazards Spring frosts; harvest rain; diseases resulting from excessive humidity.

McWilliam's Mount Pleasant Semillon

For a tour of the wineries of the Lower Hunter Valley **See pp56–57**

47

Wine Areas of New South Wales

Upper Hunter Valley

The northernmost of the well-known Hunter Valley regions, the Upper Hunter is the baby in viticultural terms. It took until 1960 for a producer, namely Penfolds *(see p37)*, to venture out of the successful Lower Hunter into this area around the farming town of Denman. However, the Upper Hunter is no longer a mere extension of its southern relative. This region has taken on a character of its own, in particular since the arrival of Arrowfield in 1968 and Rosemount Estate *(p58)* in 1969. These producers showed that white wines are the region's main strength, namely butter-rich Chardonnay and soft Semillon. Both have a rounded character and are full of plump, ripe fruit. Of the red wines, the flavorsome

McWilliam's vineyards in New South Wales

Cabernet Sauvignon has a natural juiciness, and the Shiraz, while lacking the striking individuality of the Lower Hunter version, is warm and textured. 🌿 *fertile black silty loams, red-brown duplex soils* 🍇 *Cabernet Sauvignon, Shiraz, Merlot* 🍇 *Chardonnay, Semillon, Sauvignon Blanc* 🍷 *red, white, sparkling*

Lower Hunter Valley

The Lower Hunter Valley is a wine region recognized the world over for its distinctive, archetypal Australian styles. With more than 80 wineries, Pokolbin is the region's winemaking epicenter. To its west lies the subregion of Broke Fordwich, where there are another 20 or so wineries. The area mostly follows the Hunter River, with the rugged Brokenback Range forming the western boundary.

The Lower Hunter Valley finds its greatest expression in Semillon, a white variety that is traditionally picked at low sugar levels (by Australian standards) of around 11 to 12 percent and vinified to reveal crisp delicacy and extraordinary intensity when young, but developing into a rich, complex, honeyed wine with time. The Lower Hunter's great red, of almost rustic appeal, is Shiraz. These two world-class wines are unlikely heroes in a climate that can be anything but conducive to winemaking. The Hunter is hot,

---

Hunter Valley Semillon

Traditional Hunter Valley Semillon does not appear to be much of a classic in its youth, but with age, it is a masterpiece. In fact, a young Semillon looks watery in the glass, there is a vague aromatic and lemony tang about it, and it has a striking acidity and dryness. It is unoaked and alcohols are generally on the low side. Some producers have tinkered with the style to make it more drinkable early on, but true Hunter Semillon fans buy the wine to age. Left in the bottle, it develops a golden toastiness and becomes rich and complex. The high acidity of its youth keeps the wine firm as it ages. It is not uncommon for Hunter Semillon to age beautifully for a decade or more, but it is often enjoyable after five years. The past masters of the style—McWilliam's, Tyrrell's, Lindemans—are able to point to examples that still drink superbly at 15 and 20 years of age.

New South Wales

often has rain during the harvest, and can be humid, making disease an ever-present problem. But these grapes obviously do not mind a little heat, and winemakers have discovered that the rich red soils—well-draining red clays—are highly suited to Shiraz, while the creek bed sandy loams and yellow clays are best suited to white varieties like Semillon.

The success of these grapes in the Valley attests to the vision of two main pioneering Hunter winemakers: James Busby and George Wyndham, both of whom planted vineyards here in the early 1800s. By 1843, an ex-Royal Navy doctor, Dr. Henry Lindeman—who was destined to become a household name *(see p59)*—had also planted vines in the Valley. Today, the Lindeman name graces many wines under the Southcorp banner, and is a global brand.

Of the more recent pioneers, Dr. Max Lake, founder of Lake's Folly, deserves a mention for planting Cabernet Sauvignon in 1963, a time when there was none in the Valley, and for seeing its potential as an equally earthy, savory partner to Shiraz. Murray Tyrrell of Tyrrell's *(p60)*, with similar foresight, achieved even greater recognition for Hunter Chardonnay.

🖾 well-drained red duplex and loam soils
🍇 Shiraz, Cabernet Sauvignon, Pinot Noir
🍇 Chardonnay, Semillon, Verdelho
🍷 red, white, sparkling, dessert, fortified

Mudgee

Mudgee is an Aboriginal term meaning "nest in the hills," an apt description for this hilly area on the western slopes of the Great Dividing Range, which is home to many small, family-owned vineyards. It has a very different climate to the neighboring Hunter Valley on the other side of the range. Rainfall is lower, there are

Hunter Valley Shiraz

Hunter Shiraz smells and tastes like the sun-baked earth it comes from. Perhaps the most easily recognizable Shiraz in Australia, it is definitely a different beast from the rich, peppery Shiraz found in other states. Firstly, it does not share the same intensity or power. Hunter Shiraz is medium-bodied, and even when there is no rain at harvest and the grapes ripen longer on the vine, the style is never a blockbuster. That, in turn, means the wines do not cry out for high levels of new oak. In fact, traditional Hunter Shiraz rarely sees or needs new oak. Instead, big, old oak casks provide the right environment to soften tannins and impart a little extra complexity, thus preserving all those distinctly Hunter smells and flavors.

more hours of sunshine, and most of the vineyards require irrigation. Mudgee's harvest takes place four weeks after the Hunter's. The story goes that some Chardonnay cuttings (brought out from Europe by James Busby in 1832) ended up here at Craigmoor vineyard, where they were called White Pineau. Pioneering winemaker Alf Kurtz of Mudgee Wines took cuttings from Craigmoor and planted them in 1963. Only later, when a French vine expert visited his vineyard, were they identified as an exceptional, virus-free Chardonnay. This generous, peach-melon variety was the source for many of the country's future plantings. Kurtz also pioneered a full-bodied chocolatey Cabernet Sauvignon. Although these are Mudgee's two most suited varieties, demand for strong, leathery Shiraz has seen this grape thrive here, too. 🖾 *sandy loam topsoils over clay subsoils* 🍇 *Shiraz, Cabernet Sauvignon, Merlot* 🍇 *Chardonnay, Semillon, Sauvignon Blanc* 🍷 *red, white*

McWilliam's flourishing Barwang vineyard in the Hilltops district

Orange & Cowra

Orange sits well inland from Sydney in the foothills of the 4,680 ft- (1,426 m-) high Mount Canobolas. Despite a late start to wine production in the 1980s, this high, cool area has moved quickly to establish a reputation for finely structured Chardonnays and Cabernet Sauvignons. Its greatest promoter is Rosemount Estate *(see p58)*, which was among the first to highlight the area's potential.

To the south of Orange is Cowra, a warm, dry region with a special affinity for producing lively, peach-rich Chardonnay. Rothbury Estate and Petaluma were the first to capitalize on Cowra Chardonnay

in the 1970s. Styles are far from subtle, but are very appealing.

🌧 *well-drained, red-brown clays with volcanic ash and clay loam over shale, terra rossa (Orange), loamy sand and clay with red clay subsoils (Cowra)*
🍇 *Shiraz, Cabernet Sauvignon, Cabernet Franc* 🍇 *Chardonnay, Semillon, Verdelho* 🍷 *red, white*

Hilltops

Few drinkers have heard of the Hilltops region, but one range of wines from here has had huge success: McWilliam's Barwang *(see p62)*, which took off in the 1990s. The Barwang wines are stylish and elegant, a surprise to many who assumed this was a hot inland spot. Just 50 mi (80 km) south of Cowra, Hilltops actually enjoys a continental climate with a long, even ripening period. These conditions seem particularly well-suited to making smooth, fleshy, and deep-hued Shiraz and Cabernet Sauvignon, but it is still early days. Some of the companies based in the Lower Hunter Valley, including

Allandale and Hungerford Hill (Southcorp) source grapes from here, too.  dark red granitic clays with basalt Shiraz, Cabernet Sauvignon Semillon, Chardonnay, Riesling red, white

Canberra District

The capital of Australia, Canberra is home to the Federal Parliament and a plethora of accompanying government institutions. In fact, it was government research scientists who planted many of the first hobby vineyards here in the 1970s. These were sited chiefly around Murrumbateman to the north of the city and along Bungendore Ridge and on the shores of Lake George to the east. The climate of the region around Canberra is continental, with the constant threat of spring frosts and summer droughts. Irrigation is essential for most vineyards.

For the first small producers the early years were hard—few had any winemaking experience and there was no history of viticulture in the area. Nevertheless, today, many of them have become full-time winemakers, with companies like Clonakilla, Helm, Brindabella Hills, and Lark Hill making some of the region's best wines.

In 1997, the decision by the Hardy Wine Company, Australia's second largest producer, to build a 2,000-ton winery right in the heart of Canberra brought a smile to the faces of the local winemakers. The Kamberra winery and tourist complex, along with a 620-acre (250-ha) vineyard, was recognition, at last, from one of the major producers of the area's potential for making quality wines.

Ken Helm at the Helm Winery, Canberra District

These are still early days for Canberra wines, but the whites are fine-textured with gentle aromatics, evident in the delicate, floral Rieslings. The reds tend to be elegant with fine tannin structures, such as the peppery Shiraz and opulent Pinot Noir. hard red duplex Merlot, Cabernet Sauvignon, Pinot Noir Chardonnay, Riesling, Gewürztraminer red, white, dessert

Tumbarumba

Until the early 1980s, nobody had even thought of growing grapes in this region in the foothills of the Snowy Mountains, which contain Australia's highest peaks. Traditionally, this had been grazing country for sheep and cattle. The first planting in 1982 failed, but the pioneers persevered, and today the region has more than 25 producers. The altitude of the vineyards ranges from 1,000–2,600 ft (300–800 m). This cool-climate, high-altitude area is well suited to producing Chardonnay, Pinot Noir, and Pinot Meunier for sparklings. These varieties account for more than 75 percent of the plantings and several big companies, including Southcorp, the Hardy Wine Company, and Orlando Wyndham, source grapes from here for their premium bubblies. Most wines are subsequently blended, but Hungerford Hill of the Hunter Valley has supported the region since the 1990s and gives Tumbarumba recognition on the labels of wines such as Dalliance Sparkling Chardonnay. granite, basalt Pinot Noir, Cabernet Sauvignon, Merlot, Pinot Meunier Chardonnay, Sauvignon Blanc red, white, sparkling

A vineyard was established near Yass in the Canberra District in the 1840s, but the region was ignored until the 1970s

De Bortoli's fermentation tanks in Riverina

Riverina

Riverina is Australia's second biggest wine-producing area, with 56,800 acres (23,000 ha) of vines producing 321,000 tons of fruit annually. Its forte is low-cost grapes. Growers, many with Italian heritage, settled here after World Wars I and II and now farm huge tracts of rich red earth, some up to 1,000 acres (400 ha), irrigated with water from the Murrumbidgee River. Many, such as De Bortoli, Riverina Estate, and Casella Wines, have built sizeable empires by supplying the cheap and cheerful end of the market from their vast estates. In fact, McWilliam's, one of the country's biggest producers *(see p59)*, whose Hanwood winery was started in 1877, calls the Riverina district home.

Makers here have worked hard to improve quality and concentrate fruit flavors, allowing them to move up into the premium price brackets. Generous Shiraz and full-bodied, sun-soaked Chardonnay are the all-around favorites, but since the 1990s, some producers have explored Durif (De Bortoli), Semillon (Riverina Wines), and Viognier and Tempranillo (Casella).

However, the star of the region is not a dry table wine but a golden botrytized Semillon of astonishing intensity. Riverina producer De Bortoli pioneered botrytis Semillon in 1982. Its Noble One is the benchmark, delivering marmalade, citrous peel, and sweet apricot flavors. *sandy loam over sandy clay loam* Shiraz, Cabernet Sauvignon, Mourvèdre Semillon, Trebbiano, Chardonnay *red, white, dessert*

Botrytis or Noble Rot

Noble rot is caused by a fungal spore, *Botrytis cinerea*, common in the Sauternes district of Bordeaux, which produces the world's most famous botrytized wines. The rot appears as a brown spot, which extends to cover the grape until it eventually shrivels. It reduces the grape's water content, increasing sugar levels, acidity, viscosity, and flavor to give a sweet, unctuous, aromatic dessert wine. The grapes are left on the vine for some two months after ripening and harvested selectively. This explains the relatively small quantities of wine and the high production costs. Botrytized wines are now made in many parts of the New World, including, perhaps surprisingly, the Riverina area of New South Wales.

Winemaking in Queensland

It may come as a surprise to many that subtropical Queensland has made wine since 1863. Up until the end of the 19th century, many small vineyards were planted here, but the federation of Australia in 1901 dealt the fledgling industry a near-mortal blow. Federation brought free trade between the states, which meant that Queensland's growers, who had been protected by import tariffs, could no longer compete with the large wine companies from the south.

Albert River Wines Chardonnay label

Over the last two decades, however, their fortunes have revived. Producers avoid heat and humidity by seeking out high altitudes or areas cooled by sea breezes. The Granite Belt around Stanthorpe and Ballandean in southern Queensland reaches altitudes of 2,660 ft (810 m) and produces quality Semillon and Cabernet Sauvignon, but its most consistent performer is Shiraz.

Queensland's other major wine region is the Burnett area, north of Brisbane, where the first wines were produced as recently as 1993. Altitudes are not as high here, and the hot weather makes irrigation a must. Full-bodied, creamy Chardonnay is this area's most attractive style.

Albert River Wines

Founded in 1997, Albert River Wines has Peter Scudamore-Smith, Master of Wine, making a range of well-priced wines, including a rich Chardonnay, a plummy Merlot, and an unusual red berry-charged Shiraz-Cabernet-Merlot blend matured in oak. ◈ 1–117 Mundoolun Connection Rd., Tamborine • 07 5543 6622 • www.albertriverwines.com.au ◻ ▦ red, white, sparkling, fortified ★ Cabernet Shiraz Merlot, Unwooded Chardonnay, Grand Masters' Wine Series Shiraz

Ballandean Estate Wines

This Granite Belt producer works hard to make some of the region's most consistent, full-bodied Chardonnays. Run by the energetic Angelo Puglisi, whose family began making wine here in 1931, Ballandean has a range of some 18 different wine styles, including in some years an interesting late-harvest Sylvaner. The Estate proclaims its Italian roots with "Opera in the Vineyard," a charity event staged every year in May. ◈ 354 Sundown Rd., Ballandean • 07 4684 1226 • www.ballandean-estate.com.au ◻ ▦ red, white, dessert, sparkling, fortified ★ Family Reserve: Chardonnay, Shiraz, Late Harvest Sylvaner

Rimfire Vineyards & Winery

Grown on just 30 acres (12 ha) of a 3,700 acre (1,500-ha) cattle stud on the Darling Downs, Rimfire Vineyards' high-quality Chardonnay, Verdelho, and Shiraz enjoyed great wine show success in the late 1990s. In recent times, Rimfire has widened its range, experimenting with unusual varietals, such as the Portuguese grape Touriga Nacional and a 100 percent Cabernet Franc. ◈ Bismarck Street, Maclagan • 07 46921129 • www.rimfirewinery.com.au ◻ ▦ red, white, fortified ★ Rimfire Chardonnay (oaked & unoaked)

Sirromet Wines

This no-expense-spared winery—with 344 acres (139 ha) of vineyards under Adam Chapman—arrived with a bang in 1998. The market-driven brand delivers wines in all price ranges, with sunny Chardonnay, well-rounded Shiraz, and smooth Pinot Noir. ◈ 850–938 Mount Cotton Rd, Mount Cotton • 07 3206 2999 • www.sirromet.com ◻ ▦ red, white ★ Seven Scenes Chardonnay

 Jim Laurie of Stone Ridge Vineyards, a small Granite Belt producer, caused a stir in 2003 by releasing a Pinot Noir at AUS$100 a bottle

A Wine Tour of the Lower Hunter Valley

The Lower Hunter Valley is dominated by the blue-green silhouette of the Brokenback Range. The valley is visited by hundreds of thousands of tourists annually, yet retains a relaxed country charm. Multi-million-dollar wineries rub shoulders with small, family-run enterprises, and the architecture varies from Tuscan- and Provençal-style villas to traditional Australian homesteads. The main wine hubs are Pokolbin, a town full of fine restaurants and wineries, and the old mining town of Cessnock.

1 Allandale Winery
Bring a picnic or throw some shrimp on Bill Sneddon's barbeque, savor a glass of his deliciously steely Semillon or scrumptious, food-friendly Matthew Shiraz, and enjoy the wide-screen valley vista. ✆ *Lovedale Road, Lovedale • 02 4990 4526*
• *www.allandalewinery.com.au*

2 Tower Estate
Len Evans' love of international art and antiques meshes seamlessly into a modern context at Tower Estate. Marvel at the amazing architecture, enjoy dinner in the restaurant, sample the fine multi-regional wines and even stay at The Lodge. *See p60.*

3 Pepper Tree Wines
Boasting the prettiest cellar door in the Hunter Valley, Pepper Tree Wines' complex includes a lawned picnic area, the Convent guesthouse, and Robert's Restaurant. For Merlot fanciers a visit here is a must.
✆ *Halls Rd., Pokolbin • 02 4998 7539*
• *www.peppertreewines.com.au*

Visitors' Tips

Route
This 21-mi (34-km) tour focuses on the wineries around Pokolbin.

Duration
About a day, if you stop at three or four wineries. Remember Australia's strict drunk-driving laws.

Wineries
Almost all wineries have a "cellar door" open to the public daily, and few charge for tastings. Many offer accommodation and excellent restaurants.

Tourist Information
Wine Country Visitor Information Centre
✆ *02 4990 0900 • www. winecountry.com.au*

Key

━━━ Tour route

 Preceding pages **Lower Hunter Valley vineyards with view of the Brokenback Range beyond**

4 Tyrrell's
The slab hut at the entrance is the 1850s "homestead," erected by Edward Tyrrell, the current manager's great-grandfather. Wines in all price brackets are made here, but pride of place goes to the Vat wines. Daily wine tours run from Monday to Saturday. *See p60.*

5 McGuigan Wines
This is the center for the Hunter Valley Cheese Company and a great spot to stock up on picnic food, as well as McGuigan's ripe, sun-drenched styles like the Genus 4 Chardonnay and Personal Reserve Hunter Shiraz. *See p58.*

6 Brokenwood Wines
CEO/winemaker Iain Riggs started this venture as a weekend hobby. The boutique winery produces quality Hunter Shiraz. The cellar door is totally unpretentious and boasts some exclusive releases. *See p58.*

7 Lindemans
Lindemans no longer has a working winery here, but this handsome wine museum is housed in the historic Ben Ean building. Wine exhibits date back as far as the first half of the 19th century and tastings can be enjoyed in a garden setting. *See p59.*

8 McWilliam's Mount Pleasant Wines
The vineyard is organized in easily navigable blocks, inviting picnickers and walkers to roam around this estate. Or visitors can enjoy local exotica—like emu, crocodile, and kangaroo—at the café. The wines to try are the top-level Semillons, the Merlot, and the earthy Maurice O'Shea Shiraz. *See p59.*

9 The Rothbury Estate
The striking white Rothbury Estate building is a prominent Pokolbin landmark. The cellar door offers art exhibitions and coffee or lunch at Toby's Coffee House, as well as wine tastings and the daily "Grape to the Glass" tours. The estate grounds can be used for picnics. *See p60.*

bimbadgen
E S T A T E
Hunter Valley
Semillon
2001

10 Bimbadgen Estate
Relaunched with an expanded winery-restaurant complex, this estate has a strong core range of Semillon, Verdelho, and Shiraz. This is the bold new face of the Hunter Valley, also catering for tutored tastings at the cellar door, as well as providing accommodation. ⊗ *McDonalds Road, Pokolbin • 02 4998 7585 • www.bimbadgen.com.au*

Map labels:
Greta
Campbell Road
Lovedale Road
Majors Lane
Bishop's Hill
State Forest
0 km 5

Vineyards in the Lower Hunter Valley

Major Producers in New South Wales

Rosemount Estate
Upper Hunter Valley

Murray Tyrrell may have pioneered Chardonnay in Australia, but it was Rosemount's Roxburgh vineyard, founded in 1969 by Bob Oatley, that gave the grape mass appeal. Through shrewd marketing and good winemaking, he established a faultless range of wines. Rosemount released a premium Roxburgh Chardonnay in 1984: a rich, buttery wine that was lauded as the new pinnacle of Australian Chardonnay. Rosemount is now part of the giant Southcorp, but Roxburgh Chardonnay remains one of its flagship wines. Other premium wines are now sourced from several regions, among them Mudgee (Hill of Gold and Mountain Blue) and McLaren Vale (Traditional and Balmoral ranges).

Rosemount Estate

🖎 *Rosemount Rd., Denman • 02 6549 6450 • www.rosemountestate.com.au*
☐ 🖼 *red, white, sparkling ★ Giants Creek Chardonnay, Roxburgh Chardonnay, Hill of Gold Chardonnay, Balmoral Syrah*

Brokenwood Wines
Lower Hunter Valley

Brokenwood, founded in 1970, was the dream of three Sydney professionals—including noted wine writer James Halliday—who managed to turn a weekend hobby into a respected Hunter concern. The original owners left and were replaced by a number of investors and, in 1982, CEO-winemaker Iain Riggs took the helm. He is largely responsible for the emergence of Graveyard Vineyard Shiraz as one of Australia's great reds. This wine is sourced from a single vineyard (which was once chosen as a site for a graveyard but never used), and shows a most un-Hunter-like restraint and elegance. His Semillon is warm and lemony in its youth and ages beautifully. The company's second label, Cricket Pitch, offers great value for money with its multiregional blends.

🖎 *McDonalds Rd., Pokolbin • 02 4998 7559 • www.brokenwood.com.au* ☐
🖼 *red, white ★ Semillon, Graveyard Vineyard: Shiraz, Chardonnay*

McGuigan Wines
Lower Hunter Valley

Brian McGuigan, a powerful mover and shaker in the Australian wine industry, started McGuigan Wines in 1992. Its policy is to produce easy drinking wines of mass appeal.

In 2003, McGuigan Wines joined forces with major wine processor Simeon to form one of Australia's largest wine companies. It has two wineries in the Hunter Valley: Hunter Ridge, which produces premium wines such as the Genus 4 and Personal Reserve, and Hermitage Road, where juice is shipped in from all over Australia to make some of the company's more everyday brands. McGuigan Wines is now a formidable producer of wines for the domestic and international markets. ✪ *Corner Broke Rd. & McDonalds Rd., Pokolbin* • *02 4998 7298* • *www.mcguiganwines.com.au* ☐ 🖪 *red, white* ★ *Genus 4 Old Vine Cabernet Sauvignon, Personal Reserve Hunter Valley Shiraz, Bin 9000 Semillon*

McWilliam's Mount Pleasant Wines
Lower Hunter Valley
Mount Pleasant is synonymous with Maurice O'Shea, one of Australia's top winemakers. He made wines of great elegance from Shiraz and Semillon with no oak maturation, and gave them names like Anne, Florence, Philip, and Richard. O'Shea died in 1956, but the styles he inspired remain a feature of these wines to this day: Elizabeth Semillon is the top-selling Semillon in the country, released after four to five years in the bottle and showing a warm, buttered toastiness. The flagship Semillon is Lovedale, an extraordinarily complex wine, also released with some age. The Maurice O'Shea Shiraz is a modern interpretation of an original O'Shea wine: with plenty of oak but also great finesse. ✪ *Marrowbone Rd., Pokolbin* • *02 9722 1200* • *www.mcwilliams.com.au* ☐ 🖪 *red, white, sparkling, dessert, fortified* ★ *Elizabeth Semillon, Maurice O'Shea Shiraz, Lovedale Semillon*

Lindemans and the Lower Hunter Valley
The Lindemans brand, recognized around the world, is now owned by the massive Southcorp group. It began life in the Hunter Valley in 1843, when Dr. Henry Lindeman, an English settler with a passion for the health-giving properties of wine, planted a vineyard in Cawarra with Riesling, Verdelho, and Shiraz grapes. He began exporting wines to Britain in 1858, and the company flourished under his descendants until the 1930s. After World War II, Lindemans, now a public company, acquired new vineyards to make affordable, drinkable wines, many for export. The hugely successful Bin 65 Chardonnay was launched in the 1980s in North America long before it went on sale in Australia. The Cawarra name survives on labels, but the company now has its headquarters at Karadoc in Victoria, and its presence in the Hunter Valley is limited to a museum in its old Ben Ean winery *(details below)*. However, two of Lindemans' classic Hunter Valley wines were relaunched in 2004: a Shiraz and a Semillon. ✪ *McDonalds Road, Pokolbin* • *02 4998 7684* • *www.lindemans.com.au* ☐

Poole's Rock Wines
Lower Hunter Valley
David Clarke started Poole's Rock as a personal venture, making wines that he liked to drink himself, but it has grown considerably. The focus here is Chardonnay: bright, clean, minerally, and elegant. The Cockfighter's Ghost Vineyard and brand joined the stable in 1994 as a cheery second label, and Firestick, a well priced multiregional brand, was added to the Poole's Rock portfolio in 2002. ✪ *DeBeyers Rd., Pokolbin* • *02 4998 7501* • *www.poolesrock.com.au* ☐ 🖪 *red, white* ★ *Poole's Rock Chardonnay, Cockfighter's Ghost: Unwooded Chardonnay, Verdelho*

 Lindemans also has a major winery at Coonawarra, South Australia, which produces their Reserve and Coonawarra Trio ranges **See p31**

The Rothbury Estate
Lower Hunter Valley

In 1968, Len Evans and his friend Murray Tyrrell formed Rothbury, planting a vineyard on Tyrrell's land with Hunter favorites like Shiraz, Chardonnay, and Semillon. The wines were released under single vineyard labels direct to the public, who became members of The Rothbury Society. Membership brought invitations to Evans-inspired dinners and tastings—gloriously decadent affairs—at Rothbury's multi-million-dollar winery. In 1996, the company was taken over by Mildara Blass. Without Evans, Rothbury has lost some of its shine and panache, but the arrival of winemaker Neil McGuigan in 1999 has seen quality lift. ◈ *Broke Rd., Pokolbin* • *02 4998 7363* • *www. rothburyestate.com.au* ◻ ▣ *red, white, fortified* ★ *Brokenback: Sémillon, Shiraz; Neil McGuigan Series Hunter Valley Shiraz*

Tower Estate
Lower Hunter Valley

After losing his beloved Rothbury Estate *(see above)* in a hostile takeover, Len Evans started all over again with a group of investor friends and built this magnificent winery accommodation complex in 1999. The wines, like the eclectic hotel furnishings, are very Evans, boasting strong personalities and luxurious, hedonistic styles. The winery is no longer Hunter focused, and Dan Dineen is now sourcing the best of Australia's best. ◈ *Corner Broke & Halls Rds, Pokolbin* • *02 4998 7989* • *www.towerestatewines.com.au* ◻ ▣ *red, white* ★ *Hunter Valley Shiraz, Clare Riesling, Barossa Shiraz*

Tyrrell's
Lower Hunter Valley

Tyrrell's has a deep connection with the Hunter Valley: no other wine company has the tradition, the feel for the land, or the passion and faith that Tyrrell's displays. Chardonnay, Semillon, and Shiraz are still the company's cornerstone, and they come in a variety of styles. The Vat wines – the elegant Vat 47 Chardonnay, the nutty, honeyed Vat 1 Semillon, and the earthy Vat 9 Shiraz—are examples of the Hunter at its best. There are other excellent, individual styles: from the Lost Block Semillon to be enjoyed in its youth and the sherbety Moon Mountain Chardonnay, to the fruit-packed, old-vine Brokenback Reserve Shiraz. ◈ *Broke Rd., Pokolbin* • *02 4993 7000* • *www.tyrrells.com.au* ◻ ▣ *red, white, sparkling, dessert, fortified* ★ *Vat 1 Semillon, Vat 47 Chardonnay, Vat 9 Shiraz*

Tyrrell's Vat 1 Semillon

Andrew Harris Wines
Mudgee

Andrew Harris's shrewd policy of surrounding himself with talent such as star viticulturalist Dr. Richard Smart and illustrious winemaker Frank Newman has paid off: his 730-acre (295-ha) property produces three ranges that are making his name, not only in Australia, but also in the US and Japan. The Varietal Range

---

**Other Producers in
the Lower Hunter Valley**

Belgenny *Debeyers Road, Pokolbin* • *02 9247 5577* • *www.belgenny.com.au*

Glenguin *Broke Road, Pokolbin* • *02 6579 1009*

Mabrook Estate Wines *Inlet Road, Bulga* • *02 9971 9994* • *www.mabrookestate.com*

Rothvale *Deasys Road, Pokolbin* • *02 4998 7290*

Tamburlaine *McDonald's Road, Pokolbin* • *02 4998 7570* • *www.tamburlaine.com*

Poet's Corner wine cellar

comprehensively sets out his stall, while the Reserve wines consist of full-bodied Chardonnays and Cabernet-Merlots. The Premium Range produces such medium-bodied delights as the Double Vision sparkling Shiraz. 🔖 *Sydney Rd., Mudgee • 02 6373 1213 • www.andrewharris.com.au* ☐ 🖼 *red, white, sparkling* ★ *Vision, Double Vision*

Botobolar Vineyard
Mudgee
This was one of Australia's first organic vineyards, established in 1971 by journalist Gil Wahlquist. Sheep graze on grass between the vines, copper sulfate and lime sulfur are used in sprays to keep disease at bay, and birds take care of the caterpillars and moths. Kevin and Trina Karstrom took over from Wahlquist in 1994 and continued his work. They have now ventured into low-preservative wines, but the best results remain the reds where sulfur dioxide is used as a preserver of fruit aromas and flavors and an antioxidant. 🔖 *89 Botobolar Lane, Mudgee • 02 6373 3840 • www.botobolar.com* ☐ 🖼 *red, white* ★ *Shiraz, Cabernet Sauvignon, Marsanne*

Poet's Corner Wines
Mudgee
The name of this winery is a tribute to Henry Lawson (1867–1922), the famous poet and short story writer, who grew up in the Mudgee district. Established in 1989, Poet's Corner was then bought by Hunter Valley-based Wyndham Estate (which was then taken over by Orlando in 1990; *see p35*). Orlando-Wyndham saw in Poet's Corner a chance to infiltrate the mass market with a well-priced, consumer-friendly range. It offers good everyday-drinking wines in a range of three whites (notably a zesty Chardonnay) and three reds (the smooth Shiraz is great value). A Henry Lawson range was added a few years ago, while the Montrose label shows the best of Mudgee with some top-quality wines led by a rich Black Shiraz. 🔖 *Craigmoor Rd., Mudgee • 02 6372 2208 • www.poetscornerwines.com* ☐ 🖼 *red, white* ★ *Montrose: Black Shiraz, Sangiovese; Poet's Corner Unwooded Chardonnay*

The Tyrrell Dynasty
The Tyrrell family has molded the fortunes of the Hunter Valley and the whole Australian wine industry. Third-generation winemaker Murray Tyrrell jumped his neighbor's fence one moonlit night in 1967 and "borrowed" a thousand Chardonnay cuttings to plant an acre of his own. His Vat 47 Chardonnay was the wine that brought Australian Chardonnay onto the world stage. In 1973, Tyrrell's became the first in Australia to mature Chardonnay in new, French oak hogsheads 79-gallon (300-liter) barrels. In 1979, another pioneering effort, Tyrrell's 1976 Pinot Noir, made the cover of *Time* magazine after winning the Paris Wine Olympics. Murray died in 2000, leaving his son, Bruce, a shrewd wine marketer, to carry on his legacy.

Hamiltons Bluff Vineyard
Orange & Cowra

The Orange and Cowra districts are fast developing a name for their cool-climate, sultry Cabernet Sauvignon-Merlot and Chardonnay. Some detect a European wine style emerging here: light, medium-bodied, and gently tannic. These are qualities that can be found in the produce of Hamiltons Bluff. This vineyard, started in 1995 by the Andrews family, is planted with the obligatory Chardonnay, Cabernet Sauvignon, and Shiraz, as well as Viognier, Riesling, Semillon, and Sangiovese. The Chardonnay comes in three styles: Reserve, Chairman's Reserve, and unwooded. ◈ *Longs Corner Rd., Canowindra • 02 6344 2079 • www. hamiltonsbluff.com* ◐ ▨ *red, white* ★ *Sangiovese, Canowindra Grossi Unwooded Chardonnay, Chairman's Reserve*

Barwang Vineyard
Hilltops

McWilliam's *(see p59)* bought Barwang in 1989 believing that the cool-climate area on the southwest slopes of the Great Dividing Range could have a successful future. McWilliam's was right. Barwang wines are well received for their combination of generous flavor and reasonable prices. The grapes grown here are crushed on site, then the juice is transported to the McWilliam's headquarters at Yenda. It is hard to choose between the Shiraz (elegant and spicy with plums) and the Cabernet Sauvignon (equally elegant with blackcurrant and vanilla notes). Both show smooth tannic structures and the ability to age well. Barwang Chardonnay is also beautifully restrained. ◈ *68 Anzac St., Chullora • 02 9722 1200 • www.mcwilliams.com.au* ◐ ▨ *red, white* ★ *Shiraz, Cabernet Sauvignon, Chardonnay*

Clonakilla
Canberra District

Since taking over from his father in 1997, Tim Kirk has fashioned some of the most exciting Shiraz in Australia. He blends his peppery Shiraz with a touch of the white grape Viognier to give his wine a breathtaking fragrance and translucent appearance. In fact, everything Kirk turns his hand to is a gem, from his lively Riesling to the flowery delicacy of his varietal Viognier. ◈ *Crisps Ln., Murrumbateman • 02 6227 5877 • www. clonakilla.com.au* ▢ ▨ *red, white* ★ *Shiraz-Viognier, Riesling, Viognier*

Helm Wines
Canberra District

A former scientist and expert in phylloxera, Ken Helm has been making wine here since 1973, and is a keen supporter of the emerging Canberra wine region. His winemaking reflects a purist's scientific eye and emphasizes the region's clean fruit and

---

Great Shiraz Producers in New South Wales

firm acids. This is seen in a tightly structured Cabernet Sauvignon-Merlot, an unwooded Chardonnay bristling with citrus zest, and Helm's passion: a strong lime and mineral Riesling. ◈ *Butts Rd., Murrumbateman • 02 6227 5953 • www.helmwines.com.au* ☐ ◰ *red, white, dessert ★ Riesling, Cabernet Sauvignon-Merlot, Unwooded Chardonnay*

Lark Hill Winery
Canberra District
Dr. David and Sue Carpenter first made their name in the 1980s with fresh, aromatic cool-climate Rieslings from their 2,820 ft- (860m-) high vineyard near Lake George. This was then followed by a subtl-nuanced, firm-structured Chardonnay. The 1990s brought a flagship Lark Hill wine: a powerful, rich, and velvety Pinot Noir. In exceptional years, a super-premium Pinot is produced—Exaltation (the term for a group of larks in flight). ◈ *Bungendore Rd., Bungendore • 02 6238 1393 • www.larkhillwine.com.au* ☐ ◰ *red, white ★ Exaltation, Pinot Noir, Riesling, Shiraz*

Casella Wines
Riverina
The 2001 launch of the Yellowtail range, with its easy-going, slightly sweet Chardonnay and peppery Shiraz saw Casella's sales soar. Wines from its Cottlers Bridge and Yendah Vale ranges reflect what the Riverina is best at: clean, fruity, simple wine styles at reasonable prices. Winemaker John Casella is now ready to explore the top end of the market, and has signaled his ambition by sourcing wines from areas outside the Riverina region too. ◈ *Wakley Rd., Yenda • 02 6961 3000 • www.casellawine.com.au* ◕ ◰ *red, white ★ Yendah Vale: Durif, Tempranillo; Caramar Estate Merlot*

**Yellow Tail,
Casella Wines**

De Bortoli Wines
Riverina & other areas
De Bortoli is a very successful wine empire built on the passion and hard work of Italian immigrant Vittorio De Bortoli, who arrived in Australia in 1924. Today, his grandson Darren oversees the company, now the sixth largest in Australia with an annual crush of 70,000 tons. Its wines run from the everyday Deen De Bortoli range to the extraordinary, luscious Noble One Botrytis Sémillon. Since the mid-1980s, De Bortoli has established roots in the Yarra Valley, producing premium wines like velvety Pinot Noir and an elegant Chardonnay. In 2002, it also moved into the Lower Hunter Valley. De Bortoli wines always deliver over-and-above what their modest price tags suggest. ◈ *De Bortoli Rd., Bilbul • 02 6966 0100 • www.debortoli.com.au* ☐ ◰ *red, white, sparkling, dessert, fortified ★ Noble One Botrytis Sémillon, Yarra Valley: Chardonnay, Pinot Noir*

Nugan Estate
Riverina
Since 1999, businesswoman Michelle Nugan has built a 1,480-acre (600-ha) wine empire that manages to show irrigated Riverina fruit as it is rarely seen: rich, supple, well-structured, and complex. Cookoothama Pigeage Merlot is luxurious in its fruit flavor. Frasca's Lane Chardonnay avoids ripe Riverina style, instead displaying citrus and stone-fruit overtones. And Durif becomes a wine rich in savory plumminess at Nugan. ◈ *Darlington Point Rd., Willbriggie • 02 6962 1822 • www.nuganestate.com.au* ☐ ◰ *red, white, dessert ★ Cookoothama Pigeage Merlot, Manuka Grove Vineyard Durif, Frasca's Lane Vineyard Chardonnay*

VICTORIA & TASMANIA

VICTORIA & TASMANIA

WHAT VICTORIA AND THE ISLAND OF TASMANIA *lack in size they make up for in diversity. Victoria has more designated wine areas (22) than any other state, and more producers (460 and rising). The landscape bristles with vineyards, some of them large-scale operations, others family-run smallholdings.*

Winemaking in Victoria

A sheep farmer named William Ryrie planted a vineyard in the Yarra Valley in the late 1830s, and was possibly the first winemaking pioneer in the region. However, the true father of Victoria's wine industry is arguably one Charles La Trobe, an Englishman of Swiss heritage, who was posted to Australia in 1839 to become the first lieutenant-governor of the colony of Victoria. He obviously had knowledge of viticulture and must have recognized the area's potential for winemaking. Soon, several of his friends arrived in Australia from Neuchatel to plant vineyards in the Geelong district. Unfortunately, the arrival of the vine louse phylloxera via Geelong in 1875 wiped out many of these early establishments. Those that survived, however, flourished so that by 1890, it is thought that Victoria was producing more than half of the country's wine. The industry continued to develop until the 1920s, when economic hardship resulted in many vineyards reverting back to pasture.

It was not until the late 1960s that a new confidence returned to the Victorian wine industry after more

Key

▪ Victoria & Tasmania

than half a century of decline. There was another rapid expansion in the 1990s, with vineyards being established in a huge area from the Murray River to the Southern Ocean, and new wineries built to process large volumes of grapes. The most productive viticultural area is now Northwest Victoria, and most of the giant Australian producers have wineries here. There are at least 2,000 grape growers throughout the state. Many wineries within easy reach of Melbourne have created facilities to welcome visitors.

As in most vine-growing areas of Australia, plantings of Shiraz and Chardonnay dominate the vineyards of Victoria. However, some styles are quintessentially Victorian: peppery Shiraz from the Pyrenees, the fruit-driven Pinot Noir of Mornington Peninsula, classy Yarra Valley Chardonnay, the Grampians' sparkling Shiraz,

Barrel of Victoria's luscious Muscat

and the honeysuckle Marsanne of the Goulburn Valley. Then there are the fortified wines of the Northeast: these world-class Tokay (Muscadelles) and Muscats can reach the pinnacle of flavor intensity and concentration, and are rightly regarded as national treasures.

Preceding pages **Sweep of vines in Victoria's Yarra Valley**

Pipers Brook Vineyard, one of Tasmania's most prominent producers

Tasmanian Pioneers

To the south of Victoria lies Australia's largest island and smallest wine state—Tasmania. The first vineyards on the island were planted in 1823 by an ex-convict, Bartholomew Broughton, but the Tasmanian wine industry only really got going in the 1950s when Frenchman Jean Miguet planted vines near Launceston in the north of the island. As Miguet's vines flourished, Italian-Australian Claudio Alcorso was persuaded that he might also grow grapes successfully here, and in 1958, he established a vineyard at Derwent River in the south of the island. For years, these two winemakers persevered alone in the cool growing conditions until they were joined by more pioneers, such as Dr. Pirie at Pipers Brook (see pp75 & 86). There are now more than 60 wineries in Tasmania.

Sparkling Wine Industry

The suitability of Victoria and Tasmania to the production of sparkling wine was recognized in the 1980s. The Champagne house Moët & Chandon established a facility, Domaine Chandon (see p84), at Green Point in the Yarra Valley in 1985, and in the same year, Roederer invested in Pipers Brook in Tasmania (see Jansz, p86). Seppelt Great Western's sparkling wine facility in the Grampians is the biggest of them all (see p78).

VINCENT GASNIER'S Fruity Australian Whites

1. **Cullen: Chardonnay** Margaret River *p99*
2. **McGuigan: Semillon** Lower Hunter Valley *p58*
3. **Giaconda: Chardonnay** Northeast Victoria *p81*
4. **Grosset: Chardonnay** Clare Valley *p34*
5. **Hewitson: Riesling** Eden Valley *www.hewitson.com.au*
6. **Penfolds: Yattarna Chardonnay** Adelaide Hills *p37*
7. **Seppelt: Chardonnay** Barossa Valley *p36*
8. **Taylors: Riesling** Clare Valley *p41*
9. **Leeuwin Estate: Art Series Chardonnay** Margaret River *p100*
10. **Cape Mentelle: Chardonnay** Margaret River *p98*

 With its wealth of wineries and vintners, Melbourne is designated one of the world's Great Wine Capitals (www.greatwinecapitals.com)

67

Wine Map of Victoria & Tasmania

In Victoria and Tasmania, every imaginable viticultural variable is covered. Temperatures can soar up to 108°F (42°C) on the mainland, but in total contrast, there is breathtaking chill in Tasmania, where frost can be the grape's greatest enemy. Between these two extremes exists a multitude of growing areas: the warmer climes of Northeast Victoria are the source of world-class fortifieds, central Victoria is spicy Shiraz country, and southern Victoria is the realm of Pinot Noir and Chardonnay.

Brown Brothers
Milawa Vineyard
label, Northeast
Victoria

WINE AREAS & MAJOR PRODUCERS

Northwest Victoria *p70*
Zilzie Wines *p78*

Grampians *p70*
Mount Langi Ghiran Wines *p78*
Seppelt Great Western *p78*

Pyrenees *pp70–71*
Dalwhinnie *p79*
Redbank Wines *p79*

Bendigo & Heathcote *p71*

Jasper Hill Vineyard *p79*
Wild Duck Creek Estate *p79*

Goulburn Valley *p72*

Mitchelton Wines *p80*
Tahbilk Wines *p80*

Northeast Victoria *p73*

Brown Brothers Milawa *p81*
Giaconda Vineyard *p81*
Morris Wines *p82*

King & Alpine Valleys *p73*

Chrismont Wines *p82*
Pizzini Wines *p82*

Gippsland *p73*

Bass Phillip Wines *p83*
Nicholson River Winery *p83*

Yarra Valley *p74*

Coldstream Hills *p83*
Domaine Chandon *p84*
Mount Mary Vineyard *p84*
Yarra Yering *p84*

Mornington Peninsula *p74*

Dromana Estate *p85*
Stonier Wines *p85*

Geelong *p74*

Bannockburn Vineyards *p85*
Scotchmans Hill *p86*

Tasmania *p75*

Freycinet Vineyard *p86*
Jansz *p86*
Pipers Brook Vineyard *p86*
Stefano Lubiana Wines *p87*

Regional Information at a Glance

Latitude 34–38.5°S

Altitude 49–2,625 ft (15–800 m) (Victoria); 165–690 ft (50–210 m) (Tasmania).

Topography Extremely varied, from mountain ranges to valleys and coastal plains.

Soil Red loam and volcanic soils in Victoria. Clay and peat in Tasmania.

Climate Maritime. North of the Great Divide is warm and dry. South of the Great Divide is wet and cool. In Tasmania, temperatures are lower and humidity is higher than in other Australian regions.

Temperature January average is 66°F (19°C) (Victoria); 63°F (17°C) (Tasmania).

Rainfall The annual is 25 in (638 mm) (Victoria); 41 in (1,032 mm) (Tasmania).

Wind Southern Ocean provides breezes and high humidity. Windbreaks on seaward slopes protect vines from sea winds in Tasmania.

Viticultural Hazards Drought; sea wind and frost in Tasmania.

Handpicking Chardonnay grapes in the Yarra Valley

Albury
Rutherglen • Wodonga
NORTHEAST VICTORIA
Wangaratta
•Beechworth
Chiltern •
Bright
Victorian Alps
KING & ALPINE VALLEYS

Bairnsdale
Mitchell •
Sale •
Macalister
GIPPSLAND
Murray
TASMAN SEA

Tasmania

Bass Strait

Cradle Mountain
Tamar Valley
• Launceston

Mount Ossa △
Esk

42

Gordon
Derwent
Derwent Valley

Lake Gordon
Lake Pedder

• HOBART

TASMAN SEA

0 —km— 400

Wine Areas of Victoria & Tasmania

Northwest Victoria

The Northwest is one of the great engine rooms of the Australian wine industry. Wineries that are the size of small towns dominate the flat landscape, surrounded by thousands of acres of vineyards that thrive in the region's hot conditions. Irrigation, essential in these parts, comes courtesy of the Murray River, which was first exploited for this purpose by Canadian engineers, brothers William and George Chaffey, at the end of the 19th century. The climate in this part of Victoria can be compared with that of the Mediterranean, and in between the vineyards lie orchards, and olive and citrus groves.

Grapes grown in Northwest Victoria are processed locally with technologically advanced machinery and techniques, which allows for large-scale production. Big-name producers Southcorp (Lindemans), Beringer Blass, and BRL Hardy all have winemaking operations here, which are involved in producing either boxed wine or cheap and cheerful bottled wines.

In the 1970s, Sultana and Muscat of Alexandria made up the bulk of cheap blends. Today, it is more likely to be Chardonnay, the principal grape of the region, followed by Semillon, Colombard, Shiraz, and Cabernet Sauvignon. High yields, plenty of water, and sun make big, flavorsome, and affordable wines, which have led the Australian wine invasion abroad. 🍇 *brown loamy sand* 🍷 *Shiraz, Cabernet Sauvignon* 🍾 *Chardonnay, Semillon, Colombard* 🍷 *red, white*

Sally's Paddock label from Redbank Wines, Pyrenees

Grampians

The Grampians region is home to relatively few producers, but has an amazing 5,000-ton output of fruit each year. In wine terms, the area's influence belies its size: Seppelt, part of the Southcorp group, has a truly vast sparkling wine facility here *(see box)*, where all of Southcorp's sparkling wines are blended and matured. With the exception of Seppelt, however, producers in the Grampians are small-scale vignerons.

A sparkling red wine is one of the specialties of the Grampians region. This is a bubbly with bite, made from super-ripe Shiraz grapes. Shiraz is also processed in the form of a table wine—a medium-bodied gentle giant that can be deceptively intense in the glass. 🍇 *gray-brown loamy sands* 🍷 *Shiraz, Cabernet Sauvignon, Pinot Noir* 🍾 *Chardonnay, Sauvignon Blanc, Riesling* 🍷 *red, white, sparkling*

Pyrenees

The Pyrenees takes in the quiet hamlets of Moonambel and Avoca, but there's nothing quiet about the region's robust reds. Shiraz wines from the Pyrenees are strong and minty with a spice-filled perfume. Cabernet Sauvignon is the often overlooked younger sibling but, like Shiraz, shows good ageing potential. It has taken 40 years for the region to find its real strength. In the 1960s, the first modern-day Australian winery, Château Rémy, was founded for brandy production with input from drinks giant Rémy Martin. When brandy lost ground, there was a push

Towns such as Bendigo and Mildura (Northeast Victoria) are good bases from which to explore the local wineries

toward sparklings as well as table wines. The cooler slopes of the Pyrenees ranges were explored for these sparkling wines. Chardonnay, more suited as a table wine here, with its rich textural appeal, is gradually taking over. A fuller style of Sauvignon Blanc is also made. gray-brown sandy loam ⚜ Shiraz, Cabernet Sauvignon, Pinot Noir ⚜ Chardonnay, Sauvignon Blanc ⚜ red, white, sparkling

Bendigo & Heathcote

In 1851, gold was discovered at Bendigo's Creek, precipitating a famous gold rush and period of tremendous growth in the area, both civic and agricultural. By 1864, Bendigo had more than 40 vineyards. In 1893, however, although the town was still rich and thriving, the arrival of the deadly phylloxera bug marked the end of all those vineyards.

It was not until the early 1970s that Bendigo (and the neighboring and ever-growing region of Heathcote) found its feet again, and vignerons rediscovered the region's ability to produce fine grapes for winemaking. Cabernet Sauvignon, Shiraz, and Chardonnay are the staples. The reds are

Sparkling Wine City

Seppelt Great Western *(see p78)* has the biggest sparkling wine facility in the Southern Hemisphere, producing at least 4 million gallons of bubbly annually under its own name, and as much again for other labels owned by wine conglomerate Southcorp. The first owner, Joseph Best, planted the vines and built a winery in the Grampians region *(see opposite)*, employing out of work gold miners to dig the cellars. In 1887, the second owner, Hans Irvine, imported winemakers and equipment from Champagne, and in 1918, the third owner, Benno Seppelt, helped turn the company into the giant it is today. The wine labels Minchinbury, Kaiser Stuhl, Seaview, Killawarra, Fleur de Lys, Salinger, and the truly indigenous, characterful Seppelt Sparkling Shiraz are all made in this city of stainless steel.

strong and firm with forceful tannins. Wherever there is quartz in the soil (the gold-bearing kind), it translates to a mineral quality in the wines. Chardonnay here is warm and round.  brown loamy sand, clay loam, patches of quartz gravel ⚜ Shiraz, Cabernet Sauvignon, Pinot Noir ⚜ Chardonnay, Riesling ⚜ red, white

Vineyard in the rolling hills of southern Victoria

Vineyards of Stonier Wines, Mornington Peninsula *(see p74)*

Goulburn Valley

Comparisons are often made between Australia's Goulburn Valley and the Rhône Valley in France. The varieties Viognier, Marsanne, Roussanne, Shiraz (called Syrah in France), and Mourvèdre are the main grapes of the Rhône, and they are also stalwarts of the Goulburn Valley. Shiraz has been grown here since the 1860s, Marsanne from the 1930s, while other equally robust varieties suited to the warm climate arrived later.

Good irrigation is essential to maintain vines in this hard, dry grazing country, and most vineyards follow the course of the Goulburn River, which is a tributary of the Murray. The 19th-century wineries kept close to the river at Nagambie, which has a large lake system. Two of Goulburn Valley's biggest wineries, Tahbilk and Mitchelton *(see p80)*, are sited here, and Nagambie Lakes is now a registered wine area in its own right. The Shiraz vines planted at Tahbilk in the 1860s were not affected by the phylloxera pest and are still producing grapes. A rustic smell of baked earth is strong in Shiraz and Cabernet from the valley, along with the taste of chocolate and dusty, red berries. 🟫 *red & brown sandy clay loams, gravelly quartz sand* 🍇 *Shiraz, Cabernet Sauvignon, Merlot, Mourvèdre* 🍇 *Riesling, Chardonnay, Sauvignon Blanc, Viognier, Marsanne, Roussanne* 🍷 *red, white*

VINCENT GASNIER'S TOP 10 Fabulous Dessert Wines

Victoria & Tasmania

Northeast Victoria/Rutherglen

Whites of Northeast Victoria are regarded as the entrée before a big main meal of powerful fruit, awesome tannins, and potent alcohols—otherwise known as Shiraz, Cabernet Sauvignon, and Durif (California's Petite Sirah), a regional specialty. Originally from the Rhône Valley, Durif has been grown here for decades and produces a heady, spicy mix of deeply tannic wine. Centered around Rutherglen, the area is warm to hot, perfect for the production of hearty reds and exceptional fortifieds. Muscat à Petit Grains and Tokay (Muscadelle) are some of the world's most concentrated and luscious dessert wines (see p83). These wines are classified according to quality: Rutherglen, rising to Classic, Grand, and, finally, Rare.

🖋 friable red soil, free-draining gravelly quartz sands, red alluvial loam over river gravel 🍇 Shiraz, Cabernet Sauvignon, Durif 🍇 Chardonnay, Riesling, Muscat, Tokay (Muscadelle) 🍷 red, white, fortified, dessert

King & Alpine Valleys

The King Valley vineyards, in the heart of Victoria's Alps, are planted up to an altitude of around 2,600 ft (800 m), making them some of the highest in the state. This is the home of finely structured Chardonnay and Pinot Noir, as well as more aromatic whites. Further down the valley, there's a little corner of Italy with robust reds like Marzemino and Sangiovese made with firm astringency. Cabernet and Merlot are well-suited, too, with a supple, fleshy quality and some of the deepest colors imaginable. In the Alpine Valleys near Bright, the scenery is somewhat similar, but not the wines. This is warmer Shiraz territory with the grape coming in either firm and spicy, or—from producers on the northern border at Beechworth —more savory and minerally. Durif and Marzemino grapes look promising in the Alpine Valleys, while Chardonnay from here tends to be very mellow.

🖋 fertile, deep red clay loams, sandy loams 🍇 Cabernet Sauvignon, Shiraz, Merlot, Durif, Marzemino, Sangiovese 🍇 Chardonnay, Riesling, Sauvignon Blanc 🍷 red, white

Pizzini Wines label, King & Alpine Valleys

Gippsland

Such is its sprawling size that Gippsland is usually divided into west, south, and east. The west, around Moe, is possibly the driest and warmest of the three districts (relatively speaking, for Gippsland is very much cool-climate winemaking), with enough sunshine to ripen Shiraz and Cabernet Sauvignon. The south, around Leongatha, is the coolest, the wettest, and the windiest with strong breezes whipped up from the Bass Strait. Viticulture in such a climate is demanding, but the results can be excellent Pinot Noir and Chardonnay. The east, around Bairnsdale, has a more moderate Mediterranean climate, and Chardonnay is best-suited here, although pockets of Pinot Noir and even Cabernet Sauvignon can be found. Despite its size, Gippsland has fewer than 30 wineries and produces only about 300 tons of fruit each year. 🖋 dark black loams to lighter sandy soils 🍇 Cabernet Sauvignon, Pinot Noir, Shiraz 🍇 Chardonnay, Sauvignon Blanc 🍷 red, white

Yarra Valley

Victoria's earliest vineyards were established in the Yarra Valley in the 19th century. The deadly phylloxera bug never affected vines in the valley, but the fertility of the soil declined after the 1870s, and other wine regions were better suited to making the fortified wines that became popular in Australia at the time. Wine production in the Yarra Valley ceased completely in 1921.

Modern Yarra Valley history begins in the 1960s with the revival of St. Hubert's and Yeringberg wineries. It has demonstrated a phenomenal ability to make quality wines across the board from sparkling, to Chardonnay, to Pinot Noir, Cabernet Sauvignon, and Shiraz. It is only possible to produce such a range here as this is a cool viticultural area—cooler than Bordeaux but warmer than Burgundy—with a variety of subregional climates. The further north you go in the valley, the warmer and drier the climate becomes; the further south, the cooler and wetter it is. The hillsides in the Yarra Valley are as steep as the Adelaide Hills in South Australia.

Yarra Valley Chardonnay is elegant with flavors of figs and stone fruits. Pinot Noir, in the hands of the best makers, is complex, with cherry and forest fruit flavors. Both Chardonnay and Pinot Noir are the basis of tightly structured sparklings of real delicacy. The valley is also the source of great Cabernets, noted for their fine tannins and ageing ability. Shiraz, from the better sites, is taut and elegant. *hard, red duplex, deep, highly fertile volcanic soils* *Pinot Noir, Cabernet Sauvignon, Merlot* *Chardonnay, Sauvignon Blanc, Riesling* *red, white, sparkling*

Mornington Peninsula

Any wine lover's wish-list of Australian Chardonnay or Pinot Noir should definitely include one or more Peninsula wines. This area, only rediscovered for wine in the 1970s, has moved quickly to cement its place as a top Australian region. Through the efforts of producer Elgee Park, it also pioneered the charismatic white Rhône Valley variety, Viognier, in Australia, as well as the rich Alsatian-style Pinot Gris at T'Gallant. Surrounded by water on three sides, the Peninsula is highly maritime with sea breezes providing a cooling effect on viticulture. This might help to explain why cool-climate Burgundy grape varieties, and not the normal Bordeaux ones, do best here. From its late start, there are now at least 140 vineyards and 48 wineries dotted around the Peninsula from Rosebud and Boneo in the south to Mornington in the north. *well-drained clay, fertile red volcanic, brown duplex, sandy* *Pinot Noir, Shiraz* *Chardonnay, Pinot Gris, Sauvignon Blanc* *red, white*

Scotchmans Hills, Geelong

Geelong

Unfortunately, Geelong will always be remembered in Australian wine history as the landing place for phylloxera. It was first recorded here in 1877 and brought Geelong winemaking to an end by 1882. Fast forward to 1966 when there was a wine rebirth with the arrival of Dr. Daryl, a veterinary surgeon, and Dr. Sefton, whose great-grandparents had been members of the original Swiss community that had turned Geelong into a major wine district in the 19th century *(see p66)*. To this day, the phylloxera threat is very real here,

Victoria & Tasmania

but most vineyards now use quarantine procedures and phylloxera-resistant rootstock. The modern emphasis here is on red wines: Shiraz and Pinot Noir both vie for importance. The warm inland Anakie area is especially suited to generous Shiraz, while the cooler, maritime-influenced Bellarine Peninsula is making inroads with Chardonnay and Pinot Noir. And between these areas is Bannockburn, home to an unusually gamey and complex Pinot Noir.

Pipers Brook Vineyard, Tasmania

🏔 red-brown clay loam over hard clay 🍇 Pinot Noir, Cabernet Sauvignon, Shiraz 🍾 Riesling, Chardonnay, Sauvignon Blanc 🍷 red, white

Tasmania

Growing and making wine in Tasmania is hard work. No other Australian wine state is cooler or more maritime, or has vineyards that are more prone to late spring frosts or gusty winds. Selecting sites for vine-growing is a highly specialized skill in such conditions, and trial and error has been a common feature of Tasmanian winemaking. However, the island lies on the same latitude as New Zealand's South Island (see p126), and its suitability for cool-climate viticulture has been obvious for years. In 1972, Dr. Andrew Pirie gained Australia's first PhD in viticulture with his pioneering work in identifying the Pipers Brook region as a suitable area for fine, aromatic, European-style wines. His feasibility study then created a template for the future success of Pipers Brook Vineyard (see p86), currently the island's

largest, most influential producer. With mountainous terrain in the west and central parts of the island, vineyards (and people) tend to cling to the north, east, and south coastal fringes. The north—Tamar Valley and Pipers Brook—specializes in crisp Chardonnay and highly aromatic whites like Riesling and Pinot Gris. It is also home to specialist sparkling winemakers. Selected sites on the east coast are proving excellent for Chardonnay and Pinot Noir.

Southern Tasmania, around Derwent Valley and Coal River, is extremely marginal and yet can produce fine textured Cabernet Sauvignon as well as generous Riesling, Chardonnay, and Pinot Noir. Though these areas are distinct, they are not yet officially designated as viticultural sub-regions. 🏔 deep red-brown soils, gravelly basalt on a heavy clay, ironstone, shallow, sandstone-based, dark, black peaty alluvial soils 🍇 Pinot Noir, Cabernet Sauvignon 🍾 Chardonnay, Riesling, Sauvignon Blanc, Pinot Gris 🍷 red, white, sparkling

Harvesting grapes in the Yarra Valley

Major Producers in Victoria & Tasmania

Zilzie Wines
Northwest Victoria
The Forbes family have farmed their land in Northwest Victoria since 1911; they planted their first vines in 1971, but only started making wine of their own in 1999. Incredibly, given such a late start in the winemaking business, the family now owns one of the largest vineyards in the region, with more than 1,500 acres (600 ha) under vine. Zilzie wines include the top-of-the-range Show Reserve range and the Premium Range, both of which use single varietals to produce fine wines in small quantities. A more commercially attractive range is the Buloke Reserve.
🜄 Lot 66 Kulkyne Way, Karadoc • 03 5025 8100 • www.zilziewines.com. au ◑ 🖪 red, white ★ Show Reserve Chardonnay, Show Reserve GSM, Premium Merlot, Premium Chardonnay

Mount Langi Ghiran Wines
Grampians
The main vineyards are at an altitude of 1,470 ft (450 m) below the spectacular cliff-face of Mount Langi Ghiran. From their cool-climate grapes, winemaker Trevor Mast produces a classic example of the modern Australian Shiraz: medium-bodied, clean, and fine. Mast has been an influential convert to minimal use of chemical intervention in the vineyard, as well as promoting Italian grape varieties such as Pinot Grigio

(Pinot Gris). His early training in Germany has also made him a deft hand with aromatic Riesling. He has even attracted the interest of like-minded top Rhône Valley producer Chapoutier, and now has a joint venture in place to develop Shiraz. 🜄 80 Vine Rd., Bayindeen • 03 5354 3277 • www.langi.com.au ◻ 🖪 red, white ★ Cabernet Sauvignon, Merlot, Shiraz, Pinot Grigio, Riesling

Seppelt Great Western
Grampians
Seppelt had two of the greatest Australian wine pioneers guiding its early fortunes: Hans Irvine and Colin Preece. Irvine laid the roots for sparklings in the 1890s by importing winemakers and machinery from Champagne; while Preece made the company's reputation as a serious producer of reds in the 1940s, with brand names like Chalambar and Moyston. Now part of the enormous Southcorp wine group, Seppelt Great Western's strengths remain sparkling wines *(see p71)*. These are led by flagship brands Salinger Sparkling and its red equivalent, Show Sparkling Shiraz. There is a range of Shiraz-based table wines, too. Chalambar is an everyday red, while the St. Peters Shiraz is the best red produced in the region.
🜄 Moyston Rd., Great Western • 03 5361 2239 • www.seppelt.com.au ◻ 🖪 red, white, sparkling, dessert, fortified ★ Show Sparkling Shiraz, Salinger Sparkling, St. Peters Shiraz

Seppelt Sparkling Shiraz

Preceding pages Jansz vineyards at Pipers Brook, Tasmania, with Mount Arthur in the distance

Dalwhinnie
Pyrenees

It was Dalwhinnie's Chardonnay that first attracted attention, but this producer has revealed its real strengths to be Shiraz, Cabernet Sauvignon, and, to a lesser extent, Pinot Noir. An amazing vineyard location—up to 2,200 ft (670 m) in the Pyrenees—enables owners Jenny and David Jones to produce both warm and cool grape varieties. David looks after the Pinot Noir and Shiraz himself, preferring intensive, non-conventional, French-inspired methods that deliver complex flavors. His highly concentrated premium Eagle Series Shiraz is one of the priciest reds in the state. The grapes are sourced from a tiny 3 acre (1.2 ha) vineyard and foot-crushed prior to fermentation.
Taltarni Rd., Moonambel • 03 5467 2388 • www.dalwhinnie.com.au red, white ★ Chardonnay, Cabernet Sauvignon, Eagle Series Shiraz

Redbank Winery
Pyrenees

Sally's Paddock from Redbank is the quintessential Victoria red. "Sally" is the wife of owner Neill Robb, and the "paddock" is their 10 acre (4 ha) vineyard, which is planted with five red varieties—Cabernet Sauvignon, Merlot, Cabernet Franc, Malbec, and Shiraz. Depending on their performance each year, all or some of these are used to make the elegant Sally's Paddock blend. Robb revels in low-technology winemaking, retaining an earthiness that makes his wines both original and popular. Lately, he has developed a new range, led by Sunday Morning Pinot Gris from the King Valley.
1 Sally's Lane, Redbank • 03 5467 7255 • www.sallyspaddock.com King & Alpine Valleys red, white sparkling ★ Sally's Paddock, Sunday Morning Pinot Gris, Rising Chardonnay

Jasper Hill Vineyard
Heathcote

Ron Laughton staked a claim in Heathcote in 1976, and with just two wine styles—Riesling and Shiraz—both the man and the region have become stars since. There are two distinct vineyards here producing individual wines: the 30-acre (12-ha) Georgia's Paddock and the 7-acre (3-ha) Emily's Paddock. The bold and exotic Georgia's Paddock Shiraz tends to steal the limelight, while the refined Emily's Paddock Shiraz —blended with a small amount of Cabernet Franc—has a more elegant flavor. Laughton's biodynamic approach to wine has brought him in contact with Rhône Valley maker Michel Chapoutier and the two now have a nearby vineyard planted with French and Australian Shiraz clones.
Drummonds Lane, Heathcote • 03 5433 2528 • www.jasperhill.com by appt red, white ★ Georgia's Paddock: Riesling, Shiraz, Shiraz-Cabernet Franc

Wild Duck Creek Estate
Heathcote

Duck Muck Shiraz is one of the wines responsible for creating a new breed of cult Australian wines —the so-called "new classic" styles. Big and bold, Duck Muck Shiraz has real character (with a name like that, it would have to be characterful). Made by David "Duck" Anderson, who has a delicious sense of the ridiculous, Duck Muck can have an alcohol content as high as 17.5 percent, with lashings of succulent fruit and oak to match. His other reds, Shiraz and Cabernet Sauvignon, are well made, strong, and highly individual, too. Spring Flat Rd., Heathcote • 03 5433 3133 by appt red ★ Duck Muck Shiraz, Alan's Cabernet Sauvignon, Springflat Shiraz, Reserve Cabernet Sauvignon

Victoria & Tasmania–Producers

The distinctive winery at Tahbilk Wines

Mitchelton Wines
Goulburn Valley

Now part of drinks giant Lion Nathan, the Michelton winery is in the capable hands of winemaker Don Lewis. His Blackwood Park Riesling is one of the best-value whites in Australia, and the Crescent Shiraz-Grenache-Mourvèdre and Airstrip Marsanne-Viognier-Roussanne are contemporary takes on these Old World blends. Mitchelton has now turned its sights to newcomer Viognier, while still making one of the more interesting Marsanne dessert wines, which offers up delicious honeysuckle flavors. *Mitchellstown Rd., Nagambie • 03 5736 2222 • www.mitchelton.com.au* ☐ ☒ *red, white,*

sparkling, dessert ★ *Print Shiraz, Viognier, Crescent Rhône red blend, Airstrip Rhône white blend, Blackwood Park Botrytis Riesling*

Tahbilk Wines
Goulburn Valley

Tahbilk boasts a French-inspired château and a classic mix of Rhône Valley varieties. Yet the wines are unequivocally Australian: the reds are earthy and direct, and the oak is rarely new and intrusive, while the whites are mostly unwooded, subtle, and inviting. It has been that way for three generations of Purbrick makers. Changes at Tahbilk are very low-key, like the move to a fruitier style Marsanne, and the

VINCENT GASNIER'S
TOP 10 Australian Wines for Everyday Drinking

1. **Brown Brothers: Tarrango**
   (red) Northeast Victoria *opposite*
2. **Yalumba: Unwooded Chardonnay**
   (white) Barossa Valley *p36*
3. **Evans & Tate: Shiraz**
   (red) Margaret River *p99*
4. **Penfolds: Koonunga Hill Chardonnay**
   (white) Barossa Valley *p37*
5. **Frankland: Riesling Ferngrove**
   (white) Great Southern *p103*
6. **Yalumba: Bush Vine Grenache**
   (red) Barossa Valley *p36*
7. **Coldstream Hills: Pinot Noir**
   (red) Yarra Valley *p83*
8. **Rothbury: Shiraz**
   (red) Lower Hunter Valley *p60*
9. **Peter Lehmann: Semillon**
   (white) Barossa Valley *p35*
10. **Wynns: Cabernet Sauvignon**
    (red) Coonawarra *p41*

quiet launch in the late 1990s of its current superstar, Viognier.

◈ *Tahbilk via Nagambie • 03 5794 2555 • www.tahbilk.com.au* ◻ 🚹 *red, white, sparkling, dessert, fortified* ★ *Marsanne, 1860 Vines Shiraz, Cabernet Sauvignon, Viognier, Dalfarras Marsanne/Viognier*

Brown Brothers Milawa Vineyard
Northeast Victoria & other areas

Name just about any grape variety and the odds are that this company grows it. The Browns are a family of inveterate experimenters, who have been at the forefront of working with new-wave European varieties, and who even created a "kindergarten" at their Milawa winery in the 1980s to try out grapes such as Italian Dolcetto and Sangiovese, the Spanish Tempranillo and the Rhône's Viognier. But Brown Brothers' roots are firmly based in tannic, hearty reds, and excellent fortifieds from the Northeast. Its move into the King Valley successfully explored new sparkling and white wine territory. In 2003, the first super premium wines (red, white, and sparkling) from the Patricia Vineyard in Heathcote also came on stream.

◈ *Meadow Creek Rd., Milawa • 03 5720 5500 • www.brownbrothers.com.au* ◻ 🚹 *red, white, sparkling, dessert, fortified* ★ *King Valley Barbera, Patricia Pinot Noir-Chardonnay vintage sparkling, Shiraz-Mondeuse- Cabernet Sauvignon*

Giaconda Vineyard
Northeast Victoria

The winemaking genius Rick Kinzbrunner founded Giaconda in 1985. His initial apprenticeship in California (Napa and Sonoma valleys) was influential in developing skills such as handling wild yeasts and implementing full barrel fermentation: a cream-

The Brown Family Profile

Brown Brothers *(left)* is an age-old institution in Victoria. From small beginnings in a Milawa vineyard planted in 1889 by John Francis Brown, the family-run company became one of Australia's top producers. John Brown Senior, son of the founder, devised separate roles for his own four sons: John Junior is the winemaker; Peter, the viticulturist; Ross, the marketer; while the late Roger explored new sites. The family was among the first to capitalize on export opportunities in the 1970s; to explore cool-climate viticulture in the King Valley; to produce new wines like Tarrango; and to push the boundaries with Spanish and Italian grape varieties. In the 1990s, a new generation of Browns came on board.

textured Chardonnay is the result. An Australian classic, it contains flavors of grilled nuts, charred oak, and stone fruits. Before setting up his vineyard, Kinzbrunner also did a stint in Europe with the Moueix group, and his Cabernet, Merlot, and Cabernet Franc wines employ traditional Bordeaux techniques, while both the Pinot Noir and Chardonnay make use of classic Burgundian methods. Giaconda is a boutique winery, with extremely small yields, hence supplies are limited and prices on the high side. But such is Kinzbrunner's focus on exactitude that—having decided that the 2003 vintage Chardonnay, Pinot Noir, and Shiraz were not up to the mark—he chose not sell them at all rather than risk damaging the very high reputation of his wines. A perfectionist, if ever there was one. ◈ *McClay Rd., Beechworth • 03 5727 0246 • www.giaconda.com.au* ◻ *by appt* 🚹 *red, white* ★ *Chardonnay, Nantua Les Deux (Chardonnay-Roussanne), Shiraz*

Victoria & Tasmania–Producers

 Giaconda Chardonnay benefits from ageing for five years or so— the 2004 vintage could be its best yet

Morris Wines
Rutherglen
Founded in 1859 by Englishman George Morris, this property was one of the first commercial vineyards to be established in the Rutherglen area. The old Rhône Valley grape variety Durif is a long-time Rutherglen and Morris specialty. The company's top Muscats and Tokays (Muscadelles) are also of high quality thanks to generations of Morris winemakers putting down blending material. David Morris, son of the great Mick Morris, is now the winemaker here. The laid-back country feel he gives the place makes it hard to believe that Morris Wines are part of the very businesslike Orlando Wyndham group (see p35) and indeed has been since 1970. ✎ Mia Mia Rd., Rutherglen • 02 6026 7303 • www.orlandowyndhamgroup.com ☐
🖼 red, white, sparkling, dessert, fortified
★ Durif, Liqueur Muscat, Liqueur Tokay

VINCENT GASNIER'S
TOP 10
Great Fortified Wines

1. **McWilliam's**
   Lower Hunter Valley p58
2. **De Bortoli: Liqueur Muscat**
   Riverina p63
3. **R L Buller: Fortified**
   Rutherglen p87
4. **Campbell's Winery**
   Rutherglen p87
5. **Chambers: Tokay**
   Rutherglen p87
6. **Morris Wines**
   Rutherglen above
7. **Stanton & Killeen**
   Rutherglen p87
8. **Grant Burge: 20 Year-Old Tawny**
   Barossa Valley p35
9. **Hardy's Tawny**
   McLaren Vale p40
10. **Jim Barry: Old Walnut Tawny Port**
    Clare Valley p34

Taking a barrel sample at Morris Wines

Chrismont Wines
King & Alpine Valleys
The enterprising Pizzini family, Italian settlers who came to Victoria in the 1950s, own two wineries: Arnie Pizzini is behind Chrismont, while cousin Fred runs Pizzini (see below). The cousins have extraordinarily green fingers in the vineyard as well as intuitive powers in the winery. Arnie is responsible for what is quite possibly the best medium-priced Riesling in Victoria, and with his new Italian-style La Zona range (Pinot Grigio, Rosato Mezzanotte, Barbera, Sangiovese, Marzemino, and Marzemino Frizzante) he is entering into exciting new territory, producing very drinkable wines for the table. No heavy alcohols here, just lots of smooth fruit with a touch of bitter astringency. ✎ Lake William Hovell Rd., Cheshunt • 03 5729 8220 • www.chrismontwines.com.au ☐
🖼 red, white ★ Riesling, Late Harvest Riesling, La Zona: Pinot Grigio, Barbera

Pizzini Wines
King & Alpine Valleys
In the 1990s, it was only Pizzini's white wines that impressed. The truth is that owner Fred Pizzini just needed a little more time to get his winemaking mind around his homeland Italian grape varieties—reds like Nebbiolo and Sangiovese, as well as the occasional white

such as Vernaccia. Pizzini goes for texture, depth, and complexity in his wines, which are medium-bodied and generously fruit-filled. His passion is Nebbiolo, and he is the first Australian winemaker to reveal the true hidden depths of this Italian gem. ✎ *King Valley Rd., Whitfield • 03 5729 8278 • www.pizzini. com.au* ☐ 🖪 *red, white, rosé* ★ *Riesling, Vernaccia, Sangiovese, Nebbiolo, Rosetta*

Bass Phillip Wines
Gippsland
Regarded as Australia's foremost maker of Pinot Noir, Phillip Jones has suffered for his passion. He lived in an RV while developing his vineyard, and it was 12 years before he sold his first bottle of wine. It was worth the wait though. The perfectionist in Jones looks for ridiculously low yields (a crazy average of one ton of fruit to every 1 acre / 0.4 ha) to concentrate flavor. In his hands, Pinot Noir can be strong, but also suprisingly subtle in flavor. ✎ *Hunts Rd., Leongatha South • 03 5664 3341* ☐ *by appt* 🖪 *red, white* ★ *Standard, Premium & Reserve Pinot Noir*

Nicholson River Winery
Gippsland
Winemaker Ken Eckersley rejoices in nonconformity. He does not make wines primarily to cater to people's tastes on the Australian wine show circuit (a common preoccupation among winemakers in this country) but to those after rich mouthfuls of flavor. The flagship Chardonnay, which gives full vent to oxidized characters, sometimes combined with a touch of botrytis *(see p52)*, tends to polarize opinion in wine circles. ✎ *Liddell's Rd., Nicholson • 03 5156 8241 • www.nicholsonriverwinery.com.au* ☐ 🖪 *red, white* ★ *Riesling, Chardonnay, Pinot Noir*

Muscat & Tokay Wines of Victoria
Word has gotten out about the fortified wines of Victoria, focusing on the Rutherglen area *(see p73)*. Muscat is the luscious, raisined one; Tokay is butterscotch and nutty. No other Australian region achieves the same intensity in the glass. The warm climate needed to ripen the grapes Muscat à Petit Grains and Tokay (Muscadelle) is a key factor. Another is the intense blending wines that have been stored in cellars for decades by devoted winemakers. Then there's the role of the master blender using skills handed down through the generations. Great complexity is attained through blending parcels of separate wines: young and old, dry and sweet, barrel-aged and solera-blended (like sherry), into the final wine.

Coldstream Hills
Yarra Valley
It would have been embarrassing had Coldstream not become the prestigious, praiseworthy winery it is today, because it was the brainchild of one of Australia's most famous wine writers, James Halliday. Happily, Halliday's acres have produced some excellent products (especially the French-inspired Pinot Noirs and Chardonnays). Although the idea was Halliday's, at least some of the ever-increasing bouquets of praise must be hurled in the direction of Coldstream's inspired winemaker, James Fleming, whose range of experience in the Bordeaux region of France and Sonoma Valley in California has been brought to bear on the rounded, full style of Coldstream's wines. ✎ *31 Maddens Lane, Coldstream • 03 5964 9410 • www. coldstreamhills.com.au* ☐ 🖪 *red, white* ★ *Pinot Noir, Reserve Chardonnay, Reserve Cabernet Sauvignon*

Domaine Chandon
Yarra Valley

Domaine Chandon is almost as well known for its flashy Visitors' Center as for its sparklings. More than 80,000 people each year make their way to Green Point to enjoy hot-air balloon rides and wine-tasting sessions. However, it would be a mistake to dismiss Domaine Chandon as a big-business operation that's all style and no substance. The winery is devoted to sparkling wine and produces some of Australia's finest. All of the exceptional *cuvées* are made with *méthode traditionelle*—the bottle-fermented technique used in Champagne, where parent company Moët & Chandon is based. ✆ *Green Point, Maroondah Highway, Coldstream* • *03 9739 1110* • *www.domainechandon.com.au* ☐ 🔲 *sparkling* ★ *Pinot Shiraz, Pinot Noir, Yarra Valley Brut*

Mount Mary Vineyard
Yarra Valley

Mount Mary's wines offer a truly great experience for those wine lovers lucky enough to get hold of the tiny amounts produced. Founder and winemaker Dr. John Middleton works hard to maintain high standards. His Quintet Cabernet (a blend of five red Bordeaux varieties) is the jewel in his crown—a classically structured wine built on glorious blackcurrant fruit, generous but never overstated oak, and fine-grained tannins. A wine's ability to age is an imperative for Dr. Middleton, which means his wines take years to reveal their true personality. ✆ *22–24 Coldstream West Rd., Lilydale* • *03 9739 1761* ☐ 🔲 *red, white* ★ *Quintet, Chardonnay, Pinot Noir*

Yarra Yering
Yarra Valley

Yarra Yering

It used to be said that the only traffic jams in the Yarra Valley were outside Yarra Yering when Dr. Bailey Carrodus *(see box opposite)* opened his cellar door once a year for sales. Fortunately, you can now visit any weekend to buy the doctor's excellent wines. Both his Dry Red Number One (Cabernet-Malbec-Merlot) and Dry Red Number Two (Shiraz-Viognier-Marsanne) are superb, but should never be tackled young. In 1996, Carrodus caused a ruckus by producing Australia's very first AUS $100 Merlot. This was later followed by a dry, savory red made from seven Portuguese grapes usually found only in port. This one was named Dry Red Number Three. The company also offers a fortified wine, Potsorts, which is made in the style of a traditional vintage port and is a drier wine than most Australian fortifieds. ✆ *Briarty Rd., Gruyere* • *03 5964 9267* • *www.yarrayering.com* ☐ 🔲 *red, white, fortified* ★ *Dry Red Number One, Dry Red Number Two, Pinot Noir, Underhill Shiraz*

Mount Mary Vineyard

Bannockburn Vineyards
Geelong

The former chief winemaker at Bannockburn's, Garry Farr, shunned the media, preferring to let his wines simply speak for themselves—which they did most eloquently. His successor (as of 2005), Michael Glover, is equally concentrated on the task at hand. His stated intention is, through "integrity, rigor, a hint of madness, and a minimum of hoopla", to produce wines that reflect the unquestionable excellence at the heart of the vineyard. Certainly, the Bannockburn Pinot Noir is perfumed, silky, spicy, and savory —essentially French in influence— while the vineyard's peppery, berry-fruit, Rhône-style Shiraz and sweet nutty Chardonnay are equally complex and rewarding. ✆ *Midland Highway, Bannockburn • 03 5243 7094 • www.bannockburnvineyards. com* ● 🍷 *red, white* ★ *Pinot Noir, Chardonnay, Shiraz*

Dromana Estate
Mornington Peninsula

Green-fingered Garry Crittenden has shown that the Peninsula is a truly exciting place for Chardonnay, Pinot Noir, and even Cabernet Sauvignon—astounding in such a cool climate. His Schinus range, launched in the mid-1980s, offered rich fruity wines at great prices. In the 1990s, he released a range of Italian wine styles, named "i" (for Italian), including Arneis, Dolcetto, Sangiovese, Rosato (rosé), and Nebbiolo. In 2003, he passed on the reins to his son Rollo. ✆ *25 Harrisons Rd., Dromana • 03 5987 3800 • www.dromanaestate.com.au* 🔲 🍷 *red, white* ★ *Chardonnay, Pinot Noir, "i" Sangiovese*

Stonier Wines
Mornington Peninsula

Stonier's multilayered Chardonnay and fleshy, dark-berried Pinot Noir, both standard and reserve, are consistently among Victoria's best. Little wonder that the vineyard, established in 1978 by publishing executive Brian Stonier, caught the eye of Brian Croser of Petaluma *(see p38)*; a friendly takeover was completed in 1998. Stonier (like Petaluma) is now part of Lion Nathan, but motivated winemaker Tod Dexter continues to set the Stonier style. ✆ *2 Thompsons Lane, Merricks • 03 59 89 8300 • www.stoniers. com.au* 🔲 🍷 *red, white* ★ *Pinot Noir, Chardonnay (standard & reserve)*

Dr. Bailey Carrodus

Dr. Carrodus came to the Yarra Valley in 1969 and planted 30 acres (now 69 acres) first with Cabernet Sauvignon and Shiraz, followed by the unconventional choices of Pinot Noir and Viognier. His guiding principles were to promote an elegant style of wine associated with cool-climate viticulture and to highlight the complexity that grows with maturity. His unorthodox methods have included using exclusively French oak, relatively high levels of volatile acidity (in reds), and botrytis-affected fruit (in whites). His latest move is to blend port grape varieties into a dry red.

Victoria & Tasmania—Producers

Scotchmans Hill
Geelong

It took two decades of making well-priced, easy-drinking Pinot Noir and Chardonnay before the Browne family decided in 2002 to make a statement by releasing their first reserve single vineyard wines (using the same grape varieties) from their Norfolk and Sutton vineyards. Laying-down potential has not figured strongly in the company's wines in the past, but winemaker Robin Brockett has now fashioned the reserve styles with a tighter complexity that should see them age well. Having identified the vineyard areas that produce the best fruit, Brockett's winemaking philosophy is to allow the character and quality of the *terroir* to shine through clearly in the reserves. The company's other brands—Swan Bay, The Hill, and Scotchmans Hill standard range—are more about the craft of blending, making use of grapes sourced from several areas. These brands produce reliable, early-drinking wines. ◈ *190 Scotchmans Rd., Drysdale • 03 5251 3176 • www. scotchmanshill.com.au* ☐ ◻ *red, white* ★ *Norfolk Vineyard Pinot Noir, Sutton Vineyard Chardonnay*

Freycinet Vineyards
Tasmania

Gut instinct told Geoff Bull in 1980 that a 450-acre (182-ha) parcel of land he had bought was suited to winegrowing. He planted a selection of grapes to see if he was right and almost all (with the exception of Müller-Thurgau) were successful. His son-in-law, Claudio Radenti, transformed the grapes into some of the best, most consistent wines in Tasmania. The Freycinet style is super-clean and fresh with razor-sharp fruit. ◈ *15919 Tasman Highway, Bicheno • 03 6257 8574* ☐ ◻ *red, white, sparkling* ★ *Radenti Sparkling, Chardonnay, Pinot Noir*

Jansz
Tasmania

It started in 1985 when Heemskerk, one of Tasmania's leading producers at the time, announced a joint venture with Champagne house Louis Roederer to make sparkling wine in Tasmania. A vineyard was planted especially for the task at Pipers Brook. The region has a climate very similar to that of Champagne in France, and Jansz is now considered by some to be the standard bearer of Australian sparkling wine. Winemaker Natalie Fryar concentrates on three styles of sparkling whites: the creamy vintage sparkling, released after three years ageing on lees; the sherbety non-vintage Chardonnay-Pinot Noir blend, and the late disgorged style for those who like their sparklings rich and honeyed. In addition, Fryar produces a highly regarded vintage rosé, of which the 2002 was a particularly fine year. ◈ *1216B Pipers Brook Rd., Pipers Brook • 03 6382 7066 • www. jansz.com.au* ☐ ◻ *sparkling* ★ *Jansz Vintage, Jansz Non-Vintage, Jansz LD (Late Disgorged), Premium Vintage Rosé*

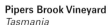

Pipers Brook wines

Pipers Brook Vineyard
Tasmania

Pipers Brook Vineyard (PBV) was long associated with one man—Dr. Andrew Pirie—and his winemaking dream *(see p75)*. That era ended in 2003, when the company was taken over by Kreglinger Australia. Future change is certain with the expansion planned for some labels, in particular the top-selling mid-level brand, Ninth Island. This company dominates the Tasmanian wine scene with more than 490 acres (200 ha) of vineyards producing quality wines that have a

Jansz winery at Pipers Brook, Tasmania

Burgundian and Alsatian bent. Aromatic varieties like Riesling, Pinot Gris, and Gewürztraminer are vibrant; while Chardonnay and Pinot Noir are supremely elegant, as is the Kreglinger sparkling, made in the style of Pirie's favorite Champagne, Bollinger.

⊗ 1216 Pipers Brook Rd., Pipers Brook
• 03 6332 4444 • www.pipersbrook.com
▢ West Tamar 🍷 red white, sparkling
★ Ninth Island, Kreglinger, Riesling, Summit Chardonnay, Pinot Noir

Stefano Lubiana Wines
Tasmania

Stefano Lubiana's move to Hobart, Tasmania, brought him national recognition when he began

producing elegant sparkling wines, Pinot Noir, and Chardonnay. In one of Australia's coldest wine regions, he manages to achieve incredibly ripe fruit with alcohol levels of up to 14.5 percent, which is transformed into some of Tasmania's most complex wines. Any wine made by Lubiana is highly individual in style, and none more so than his full-bodied Pinot Grigio. First made in 2000, the 2005 vintage is the best yet—drink it from now until 2009. ⊗ 60 Rowbottoms Rd., Granton • 03 6263 7457
• www.stefanolubiana.com ▢ 🍷 red, white, sparkling ★ Sparkling Brut Non-Vintage, Primavera Chardonnay, Primavera Pinot Noir, Pinot Grigio

---

Other Producers in Victoria & Tasmania

Campbell's (Rutherglen)
Murray Valley Highway • 02 6032 9458
• www.campbellswines.com.au

Chambers (Rutherglen)
Rosewood Winery, Rutherglen
• 02 6032 8641

Chapoutier (Grampians & other areas)
477 Bridge Road, Richmond
• 03 9429 8301
• www.mchapoutieraustralia.com

Charles Melton Wines (Barossa Valley)
Krondorf Rd, Tanunda • 08 8563 3606
• www.charlesmeltonwines.com.au

Métier Wines (Yarra Valley & other areas)
440 Healesville Road, Yarra Glen
• 0419 678 918

No Regrets (Tasmania)
40 Dillons Hill Road, Glaziers Bay
• 03 6295 1509

R L Buller & Son (Rutherglen)
Three Chain Road, Rutherglen
• 02 6032 9660

Stanton & Killeen Wines (Rutherglen)
Jacks Road, Rutherglen
• 02 6032 9457
• www.stantonandkilleenwines.com.au

Wellington (Tasmania)
489 Richmond Road, Cambridge
• 03 6248 5844

Yarra Burn (Yarra Valley)
60 Settlement Road,
Yarra Junction
• 03 5967 1428
• www.yarraburn.com.au

Yering Station (Yarra Valley)
38 Melba Highway, Yarra Glen
• 03 9730 0100
• www.yering.com

WESTERN AUSTRALIA

WESTERN AUSTRALIA

| N THIS STATE OF SUN-SEARED PLAINS *and rugged mountain ranges, it is incredible that a wine industry has not only survived but flourished. This has been achieved by keeping to the temperate south and focusing on land suitable for viticulture around the capital Perth and other coastal settlements. Only a few vineyards are sited inland away from the direct cooling influence of the sea.*

Western Australia (or WA) may be vast, but only 28,000 acres (11,400 ha) of it are actually under vine at present, yielding less than 7 percent of Australia's total wine output. However, it is the quality rather than the quantity that counts here.

In the 1920s, the emergence of luscious fortified wines from the hot Swan District just north of Perth revealed that the region had real possibilities for wine, but it was Houghton Wine Company's 1930s "White Burgundy"—a flavorful golden white—which really put Western Australia on the wine map. In 2005, Houghton's announced that the wine, still being made after 60 years, would from now on be known as "White Classic."

In the end, however, it was not to be rich, sweet ports and sherries or imitation Burgundy that would be the making of Western Australia's wine industry. The state's current wine boom was kick-started some 30 years later by a 1965 research report *(see p94)* that highlighted Margaret River as an exciting new wine area—similar in climate and growing conditions to Bordeaux. Ten years later, 11 vineyards had already been planted there, and

Key

Wine areas of Western Australia

the rest is history. Today, Margaret River stands as Western Australia's pre-eminent wine region, although a number of promising new viticultural areas like Great Southern could be set to rival it in the future.

It is perhaps ironic that wines produced from traditional French grapes such as Cabernet Sauvignon, Shiraz, and Semillon should have had such success in this corner of Australia. In the Napoleonic era, two French ships under the command of Nicolas Baudin were sent to explore the South Seas, reaching the coast of the Margaret River region in 1801. Geographical features here still have French names—Cape Naturaliste and Geographe Bay were named after Baudin's ships. The French, however, did not try to colonize the area, otherwise it might be called Terre Napoléon, the name given to it by Baudin, and the wine industry today might have quite a different character.

Shiraz grapes

Climate and Terrain

The climate of Western Australia's wine areas varies enormously—from very hot, dry summers and wet winters in the Swan Valley in the north, to the Mediterranean climate of Margaret River, and the cooler

 Preceding pages **Vineyard in Margaret River, Western Australia's most successful wine region of the past 30 years**

Vineyards near Mount Barker in the remote Great Southern region

Great Southern area in the south. Most of the state's vineyards are planted on well-drained sandy or gravelly topsoil, which means that drip irrigation is usually necessary during the summer. Conversely, as the subsoil tends to be clay, and winters can be very wet, growers often have problems with waterlogging. Most vineyards have been established on the flat coastal plain and valley floors, and machine harvesting is favored. However, imaginative growers are looking at the hillier areas around Denmark and Mount Barker, which have great potential.

Chardonnay, Sauvignon Blanc, Semillon, and, increasingly, Riesling are the most planted white varieties. The state has been successful with Bordeaux reds, too—Cabernet Sauvignon, Merlot, and Cabernet Franc— producing some world-class examples. However, it is Shiraz that is gaining most recognition, with cool-climate examples showing a highly attractive spicy pepperiness and a new exciting weight that is rare in Australian reds and marks these wines—and Western Australia—as world class.

In a Class of its Own

The subtle qualities of many Western Australian wines may come as something of a surprise. Unlike the mainstream bold Australian style, they tend to be generous in fruit flavor, medium- rather than full-bodied, and supported by an ultrafine structure.

VINCENT GASNIER'S TOP 10 Great Cabernet Sauvignons

1 **Vasse Felix**
  Margaret River *p100*
2 **Katnook (Wingara)**
  Coonawarra *p41*
3 **Coonawarra Estate**
  Coonawarra *p41*
4 **Wynns Majella**
  Coonawarra *p41*
5 **Hollick**
  Coonawarra *p41*

6 **Cape Mentelle**
  Margaret River *p98*
7 **Moss Wood Winery**
  Margaret River *p100*
8 **Leeuwin Estate**
  Margaret River *p100*
9 **Cullen Wines**
  Margaret River *p99*
10 **Xanadu Wines**
  Margaret River *p101*

Western Australia

Wine Map of Western Australia

*Western Australia may be the largest state in the country, but in wine terms,
it is a mere minnow. With the exception of those in the blazingly hot Swan
District, wineries tend to be concentrated mostly south of the capital, Perth.
They hug the coastal areas, where the sea breezes keep temperatures
sufficiently cool to produce fine wines, especially in the prime vine-growing
area of Margaret River. Regional differences have started to reveal
themselves: the emerging Pinot Noirs of Pemberton and Manjimup, the*
*Rieslings of Mount Barker, and the Shiraz and Cabernet Sauvignons of Great
Southern are now among the most exciting wines produced in the state.*

32

WINE AREAS & MAJOR PRODUCERS

Geographe *p96*

Swan District *p94*
Houghton Wine Company *p98*
Sandalford Wines *p98*

Pemberton *p96*
Picardy *p102*
Smithbrook Wines *p102*

Margaret River *pp94–95*
Cape Mentelle *p98*
Cullen Wines *p99*
Evans & Tate *p99*
Fermoy Estate *p99*
Howard Park Wines *p100*
Leeuwin Estate *p100*
Moss Wood Winery *p100*
Vasse Felix *p100*
Voyager Estate *p101*
Xanadu Wines *p101*

Manjimup *pp96–7*
Chestnut Grove Wines *p102*
Stone Bridge Estate *p102*

Great Southern *p97*
Alkoomi Wines *p102*
Frankland Estate *p103*
Plantagenet Wines *p103*
Wignalls Wines *p103*

INDIAN OCEAN

33

Cape
Naturaliste

Geographe
Bay

Busselton

MARGARET
RIVER

Margaret

34

Margaret
River

Cape
Leeuwin

Western Australia's prime viticultural area, Margaret River

SWAN
DISTRICT

ERTH

Swan

mantle

Canning

Rockingham

Darling

Peel
Inlet

Range

Murray

Bunbury

Collie

Collie

tratham

Wellington
Reservoir

GEOGRAPHE

Blackwood

Regional Information at a Glance

Latitude 30–35°S.

Altitude 130–1,300 ft (40–400m).

Topography Flat alluvial river plains, hills and ridges.

Soil Sandy and gravelly loams with overlying clay or granite of moderate fertility. Swan River irrigates the less fertile sandy soil in Swan District.

Climate Maritime; the growing season is lengthened by reduced diurnal and seasonal temperature fluctuations. Swan District and Great Southern are the hottest,

driest parts of the state, and irrigation remains a priority in these regions.

Temperature January average is 70°F (20.5°C).

Rainfall Annual average is 45 in (1,145 mm).

Wind Sea breezes moderate temperatures. Swan District: cooling afternoon wind called the "Fremantle Doctor." Great Southern: cold Antarctic current brings icy winds known as the "Roaring Forties."

Viticultural Hazards Wind damage; birds; drought.

Hand-picking grapes in a Margaret River vineyard

Tone

Manjimup

Warren

PEMBERTON

MANJIMUP

Pemberton

Lake
Muir

FRANKLAND
RIVER

Stirling Range

GREAT
SOUTHERN

MOUNT
BARKER

Mount
Barker

PORONGURUP

Frankland

Old Kent

Denmark

DENMARK

ALBANY

Albany

35

SOUTHERN OCEAN

0 — km — 50

Wine Areas of Western Australia

Swan District

The Western Australian wine industry was born in the Swan District in 1829. Olive Farm at Guildford, north of Perth, has the distinction of being the site of the first vineyard, but it is the Houghton Wine Company *(see p98)* that is recognized as marking the start of the commercial wine industry here. Its first vineyard in the Swan Valley was planted as early as 1836, but it did not produce any wine for sale until 1859, and even then it only amounted to 25 gallons.

The subregion Swan Valley is one of the hottest winemaking regions in the world, making it perfect for the production of the luscious fortified wines that came to prominence in the 1920s. Other wine styles then followed in the 1930s—tending to be full-bodied with a soft, mouth-filling generosity. The best areas of the Swan Valley are cooled by the famous wind, known as the "Fremantle Doctor," for which the inhabitants of Perth are so grateful on summer afternoons. Although the heat has led to a number of vineyards falling in recent years, the search for higher, cooler areas,

such as Moondah Brook in the north, has definitely been rewarded with some high-quality wines, like Verdelho and Chenin Blanc. *yellow-brown loamy soil, sandy yellow duplex* *Grenache, Shiraz, Cabernet Sauvignon* *Chenin Blanc, Chardonnay, Verdelho* *red, white, fortified*

Margaret River

The Margaret River area has it all: sunshine, surf, and world-class wines. The star of Western Australia's wine regions, Margaret River is one of the most maritime-influenced regions in the country, comprising a coastal strip of low ridges from Cape Naturaliste in the north to Cape Leeuwin in the south. The river from which the region takes its name flows west through its center to the ocean. The promontory is open to the ocean on three sides, with winds from the Indian Ocean moderating its warm climate.

In 1965, Dr. John Gladstones, an agronomist, put forward the tantalizing theory that Margaret River had the potential to become Australia's Bordeaux. He found close climatic similarities between this remote corner of Australia and the celebrated St.-Émilion and Pomerol districts of Bordeaux. Amazingly, where there were some differences, it was Margaret River that had the edge over Bordeaux, with more reliable summer sun, while there was much less risk of its being assaulted by spring frosts or by excessive amounts of rain during ripening.

Voyager Estate's winery in Margaret River

Sandalford vineyard in Western Australia's Swan District

Just as Gladstones predicted, the region did indeed have a strong affinity with Bordeaux, and since 1967, when it had just one vineyard (Vasse Felix, *p100*), Margaret River has gone from strength to strength. In the 1970s, 20 new vineyards were established, another 23 were planted in the 1980s, and there are now more than a hundred producers in the region. It was Margaret River that established Australia's first Appellation of Origin system in 1978.

The principal red grape varieties of Bordeaux—Cabernet Sauvignon, Merlot, Cabernet Franc, and Petit Verdot—all excel in this region. The wines they produce are generous in fruit and smooth in tannin but also well-structured. Indeed, the words most often employed to describe Margaret River Cabernet are "stylish and elegant." Sauvignon Blanc and Semillon, the traditional white varieties of

Bordeaux, have also adapted well here, both as varietals and combining to produce Margaret River's signature Semillon-Sauvignon blend. Producers have also succeeded in creating a creamy, complex Chardonnay.

One rather unusual problem faced by Margaret River's grape growers are the parrots, although sunflowers seem to distract them from the vines. 🟫 *gravelly sandy loams with underlying granite* 🟦 *Cabernet Sauvignon, Shiraz, Merlot, Cabernet Franc, Pinot Noir, Petit Verdot* 🟦 *Chardonnay, Semillon, Sauvignon Blanc, Riesling* 🟥 *red, white*

VINCENT GASNIER'S TOP 10 Star Sauvignon Blanc Producers

1. **Nepenthe Wines** Adelaide Hills *p41*
2. **Fermoy Estate** Margaret River *p99*
3. **Stafford Ridge** Adelaide Hills *p41*
4. **Shaw & Smith** Adelaide Hills *p39*
5. **Preece** Goulburn Valley www.preece.com.au
6. **Nick Faldo (Wingara)** Coonawarra *p41*
7. **Katnook (Wingara)** Coonawarra *p41*
8. **Petaluma: Bridgewater Mill** Adelaide Hills *p38*
9. **Howard Park Wines** Margaret River *p100*
10. **Smithbrook** Pemberton *p102*

The family-run Picardy winery in Pemberton

Geographe

This area takes its name from Geographe Bay, a popular seaside resort. While grapes have been cultivated here since the 1920s, the modern resurgence of the area on the wine scene dates back to 1973 when Dr. Barry Killerby established Leschenault Wines (now Killerby Wines) at Stratham, close to the Indian Ocean. He was followed by Capel Vale in 1975, and these two producers still dominate this coastal strip north of Margaret River. The climate is warm and dry, yet influenced by ocean breezes that have a cooling and humidifying effect on the vineyards. The region has four rivers, the Capel, the Collie, the Ferguson, and the Harvey, which have contributed to the quality of the soil over the centuries. Chardonnay is the most consistent performer and it runs the gamut of styles from fine to full-bodied. New red stars on the rise are robust Shiraz and full-bodied Merlot.
🗺 free-draining sands over limestone, sandy loams 🍇 Shiraz, Merlot, Cabernet Sauvignon 🍇 Chardonnay, Semillon, Sauvignon Blanc 🍷 red, white

Plantagenet Wines, Great Southern

Pemberton

Like Margaret River, Pemberton has agronomist Dr. John Gladstones to thank for highlighting its grape-growing potential. His report declared Pemberton to be one of the state's better sites for Pinot Noir and Chardonnay as a result of its relatively low temperatures, reduced sunshine hours, and high rainfall and humidity. His assessment has been proven correct. Site selection is vitally important in Pemberton because of its generally cool climate. The most consistent and successful wine of the area is Chardonnay. Pinot Noir has put in the odd great performance, but lacks general consistency. The low-lying mountains, northeast of Pemberton, where Salitage and Picardy have vineyards, is showing great potential for elegant, medium-bodied wines. This is place to watch. 🗺 gravelly sands & loams, fertile karri loams 🍇 Cabernet Sauvignon, Pinot Noir, Merlot 🍇 Verdelho, Chardonnay, Sauvignon Blanc 🍷 red, white

Manjimup

It is still early days in Manjimup, a wine region immediately north of Pemberton that only dates from the late 1980s. Before that it was included within Pemberton, but it has different soil and climate, being warmer with more sun and less humidity. Vineyards are pretty thin on the ground and most are run as small family concerns. The only sizeable player in Manjimup is

Cape Mentelle *(see p98)*, a Margaret River producer that set up a joint venture in 1998 with Fonty's Pool Farm, a local grower. The venture is producing a range of well-priced wines (Chardonnay, Pinot Noir, and Shiraz). Other producers are demonstrating that the region has great potential as a source of quality Chardonnay and Pinot Noir grapes as the basis for exciting sparkling wines made by the *méthode champenoise.* Others are creating some vibrantly fruity still wines led by exuberant Verdelho and easy-drinking Chardonnay in the whites, and smooth Pinot Noir and Merlot in the reds. 🗺 *gravelly sands & loams* 🍇 *Cabernet Sauvignon, Pinot Noir, Merlot, Shiraz* 🍷 *Chardonnay, Verdelho* 🥂 *red, white, sparkling*

Great Southern

Here, the emphasis is on "Great," for this is the biggest wine region in Western Australia. It is also the coolest, but has a lower rainfall then Margaret River. Great Southern has five subregions now developing individual styles. Frankland River, a small area in the west, actually has four rivers running through it, the Frankland, Tone, Kent, and Gordon. It is gaining a reputation for elegant Riesling and Cabernet Sauvignon. Mount Barker, to the southeast of

Frankland, has a Mediterranean climate and vines grow on the slopes of the hills up to 820 ft (250 m) above sea level rather than on the flat valley floors where the soil is too salty. The region produces good limey Rieslings, elegant Cabernet Sauvignons, and a delightful spicy Rhône-style Shiraz. Albany, in the south, also has a Mediterranean climate, cooled by its own sea breeze, the "Albany Doctor." The most successful winemaker there, Wignalls Wines, produces good Pinot Noir with Cabernet Sauvignon, Sauvignon Blanc and Chardonnay also performing well.

Denmark, to the west of Albany, is Great Southern's newest subregion. The area is named after an English naval surgeon Dr. Alexander Denmark and has wet winters followed by warm or hot summers. There are large plantings of Chardonnay and Pinot Noir, producing fragrant whites and juicy reds. Great Southern's fifth subregion, Porongurup, is dominated by the Porongurup Range of hills and is the latest up-and-coming region, showing promise with aromatic Riesling, generous Chardonnay, and opulent Pinot Noir. 🗺 *hard, mottled yellow duplex* 🍇 *Cabernet Sauvignon, Shiraz, Pinot Noir* 🍷 *Chardonnay, Riesling, Sauvignon Blanc* 🥂 *red, white*

Frankland Estate vineyard in the Great Southern region

Houghton's vineyard in the Swan District

Major Producers in Western Australia

Houghton Wine Company
Swan District

Legendary winemaker Jack Mann established Houghton with his sherry styles and a big, ripe Chenin Blanc called White Burgundy. Created in 1937 and still selling well, this became one of the most successful Australian wine brands of all time. Houghton's success saw a takeover by Thomas Hardy & Sons (now BRL Hardy) in 1976. The company's Jack Mann Cabernet oozes vibrant plum, while the velvety Margaret River Cabernet, from Houghton's premium regional selection, delivers flavors of blackcurrant with underlying oak-defined spices.

🌐 *Dale Rd., Middle Swan • 08 9274 5100*
• www.houghton-wines.com.au 🚪
📷 *red, white, sparkling, dessert, fortified*
★ *Pemberton Chardonnay, Jack Mann Cabernet Sauvignon, Margaret River Cabernet Sauvignon*

Sandalford Wines
Swan District

During the late 1970s and early 1980s, with winemaker Dorham Mann (son of Houghton's Jack Mann) at the helm, Sandalford dominated the wine shows and his Riesling, Chenin Blanc, Verdelho, and Cabernet Sauvignon had huge consumer appeal. Mann retired and competition saw the company's market share dwindle and it was sold, and sold again. The Sandalford name isn't as big as it used to be, but its Element range is a strong all-rounder (from creamy Chardonnay to soft, fruity Cabernet-Shiraz), while its fortifieds led by Sandalera—made from old Verdelho vines and similar to a sweet Madeira—are sensational.

🌐 *3210 West Swan Rd., Caversham*
• 08 9374 9374 • www.sandalford. com
🚪 📷 *red, white, dessert, fortified*
★ *Element Chardonnay, Element Cabernet-Shiraz, Sandalera*

VINCENT GASNIER'S
TOP 10 Wines for Storing

1. **Henschke: Hill of Grace Shiraz** (red) Eden Valley *p38*
2. **Penfolds Grange** (red) Barossa Valley *p37*
3. **Brokenwood: Shiraz** (red) Lower Hunter Valley *p58*
4. **Wendouree: Shiraz** (red) Clare Valley *p34*
5. **Glaetzer: Godolphin** (red) Barossa Valley *p34*
6. **Giaconda: Cabernet Sauvignon** (red) Northeast Victoria *p81*
7. **Leeuwin: Art Series Chardonnay** (white) Margaret River *p100*
8. **Cape Mentelle: Cabernet Sauvignon** (red) Margaret River *right*
9. **Métier: Pinot Noir** (red) Yarra Valley *p87*
10. **Torbreck: Runrig** (red) Barossa Valley *p36*

Cape Mentelle
Margaret River

The sister company of Cloudy Bay (see p130) in New Zealand, Cape Mentelle was founded in 1971 in the belief that Margaret River and Cabernet Sauvignon were made for each other. Owner-cum-winemaker David Hohnen was proved right in the 1980s with back-to-back wins of the coveted red wine

Western Australia–Producers

trophy, the Jimmy Watson. Cabernet Sauvignon is definitely the flagship here in a strong red wine stable. Inspired by his time in California, Hohnen pioneered Zinfandel in Australia and makes a particularly intense style. Cape Mentelle's Semillon-Sauvignon Blanc blend is very zesty, while its Chardonnay is wonderfully fruit-focused, and its well-structured, black-fruit Cabernet is laced with oak-derived coffee and vanilla. Veuve Clicquot invested in Cape Mentelle in 1988, but still lets Hohnen call the shots. In 1998, the company released a new brand from Manjimup, Fonty's Pool. ◈ *Wallcliffe Rd.* • *08 9757 0888* • *www.capementelle.com.au* ▢ *by appt* ▧ *red, white* ★ *Cabernet Sauvignon, Chardonnay, Semillon-Sauvignon Blanc*

Cullen Wines
Margaret River
If Australia has a premier boutique winemaker, it is Cullen Wines. The family's touch is magical, whether in their subtle Semillon-Sauvignon Blanc or in the complex power of their iconic Cullen Cabernet Sauvignon-Merlot. Dr. Kevin Cullen established the vineyard in 1971 in what was then one of the most remote winemaking regions in Australia. When his medical practice proved too time-consuming, he handed winemaking duties over to his wife, Di. When daughter, Vanya, took over in 1989, experimentation increased, and her refining of the Chardonnay in particular has led to its worldwide recognition. It is not only richly complex, but so finely structured and balanced that it is one of the few Australian Chardonnays worthy of cellaring for a decade. ◈ *Caves Rd., Cowaramup* • *08 9755 5277* • *www.cullenwines.com.au* ▢ ▧ *red, white* ★ *Cabernet Sauvignon-Merlot, Chardonnay, Semillon-Sauvignon Blanc*

Evans & Tate
Margaret River
This grande dame of Margaret River wine producers never takes its eye off the quality of the grapes it acquires from contract growers, and it shows. Franklin Tate, who has run the outfit since 1992, has raised its profile with a three-tiered portfolio—the classy Redbrook range, the Margaret River range, and the Gnangara range, named after the Tate family's first vineyard in the Swan Valley. All three include a spicy, fruity Shiraz with well-balanced tannins and a creamy oaked Chardonnay. ◈ *Metricup Rd., Wilyabrup* • *08 9755 6244* • *www. evansandtate.com.au* ▢ ▧ *red, white, sparkling* ★ *Redbrook Chardonnay, Margaret River Shiraz, Margaret River Cabernet Merlot, Gnangara Shiraz*

Fermoy Estate
Margaret River
When the Fermoy vineyard was established in 1985, it was planted mainly with Cabernet Sauvignon and Semillon with small parcels of other classic French grape varieties. When the first vintage was completed in 1988, the Cabernet Sauvignon was soon recognized as something special, showing the classic Margaret River qualities of great depth, complex aromas, and tremendous scope for ageing. Cabernet Sauvignon still heads Fermoy's list of varietals, which includes a crisp, well-balanced Sauvignon Blanc. There is now also a Reserve Cabernet, which is blended with small quantities of Merlot and Malbec grapes. The Reserve Semillon is barrel-fermented with Sauvignon Blanc added after racking. ◈ *Cowaramup* • *08 9755 6285* • *www.fermoy.com.au* ● ▧ *red, white* ★ *Sauvignon Blanc, Reserve Cabernet, Semillon*

Howard Park Wines
Margaret River & Great Southern

Jeff and Amy Burch started their wine business in Denmark in the Great Southern district in 1986 before acquiring a second winery in Margaret River. Star of the Howard Park range of varietals has usually been the rich, dark, fleshy Cabernet Sauvignon, its complexity heightened by the use of French oak. A recent success has been the lively Sauvignon Blanc first released in 2003, which bursts with tantalizing tropical fruit. Howard Park also produces fine single-vineyard wines from the Leston vineyard in Margaret River and Scotsdale in Great Southern, plus the MadFish range of easy-drinking, fruit-filled wines. This label takes its name from Mad Fish Bay on the Great Southern coast, so called because when two tides meet there, the fish in the bay jump out of the water.
Miami Road, Cowaramup • 08 9756 5200 • www. howardparkwines.com.au ☐ 🖬 *red, white ★ Howard Park: Sauvignon Blanc, Cabernet Sauvignon, Chardonnay*

Leeuwin Estate
Margaret River

The brainchild of Perth business couple Denis and Tricia Horgan, Leeuwin Estate was originally bought in 1969 as a cattle farm. But a meeting with Californian wineman Robert Mondavi in 1973 changed all that and a grand plan was hatched. Leeuwin's Art Series Chardonnay is extraordinary in fruit intensity and one of the few Australian Chardonnays to age well; it is rightly regarded as one of the best in the land. Leeuwin Estate's other wines tend to be dwarfed in its shadow, but the fine-tannined Art Series Cabernet Sauvignon and the delicate, lemony Riesling both deserve greater recognition. *Stevens Rd. • 08 9757 6253 • www.leeuwinestate. com.au* ☐ 🖬 *red, white ★ Art Series: Chardonnay, Cabernet Sauvignon, Riesling*

Moss Wood Winery
Margaret River

Winemaker Keith Mugford came to Margaret River supposedly for the surfing yet ended up staying for the wine. He has never sought the limelight, but his wines have become classics nonetheless. He bought Moss Wood in 1985 and since then has crafted Chardonnay, Semillon, Pinot Noir, and Cabernet Sauvignon to an astonishingly consistent level of quality. Moss Wood's star is its ripe berry Cabernet Sauvignon which has been modified over the years with Cabernet Franc, Merlot, and Petit Verdot. Many new releases come from their Ribbon Vale vineyard, also in the Margaret River region. *Metricup Rd., Wilyabrup • 08 9755 6266 • www. mosswood.com.au* ☐ *by appt* 🖬 *red, white ★ Cabernet Sauvignon-blend, Chardonnay, Semillon*

Moss Wood Winery Cabernet Sauvignon

Vasse Felix
Margaret River

Tom Cullity, a Perth cardiologist with the viticultural passion of a true visionary, started Vasse Felix in 1967, making him Margaret River's first commercial wine producer. In 1987, it was bought by millionaire Robert Holmes à Court. The injection of money into the winery and fine restaurant has contributed to its pre-eminent status. It is hard to say whether it is the sweet-berried Shiraz that impresses most or the Heytesbury Cabernet Sauvignon blend. In a great year, the Heytesbury shines with a good fruit generosity, softness, and elegant Margaret River herbals. There is also the top-of-the-line creamy Heytesbury Chardonnay and the impressive honeyed Noble Riesling. ✎ *Harmans Rd. South, Cowaramup • 08 9756 5000 • www.vassefelix. com.au* ☐ ▣ *red, white, sparkling, dessert ★ Heytesbury: Cabernet Sauvignon, Chardonnay, Shiraz*

Voyager Estate
Margaret River

Voyager Estate is owned by multi-millionaire mining magnate, Michael Wright. Said to be virtually teetotal, he is very serious about wine and has spent large sums on making Voyager Estate a regional landmark, both in architecture (it is very Cape Dutch) and premium wine quality. The groundwork was laid by Stuart Pym, a talented winemaker who set the style for Voyager Chardonnay—elegant, rich, and textural. The company also makes a serious barrel-fermented Semillon-Sauvignon Blanc, called Tom Price. Current winemaker

Cliff Royle shows a deft hand with oak, noticeable in both the peppery Shiraz and the tightly structured Cabernet Sauvignon. ✎ *Stevens Rd. • 08 9757 6354 • www.voyagerestate. com.au* ☐ ▣ *red, white ★ Chardonnay, Tom Price Semillon-Sauvignon Blanc, Cabernet Sauvignon*

Xanadu Wines
Margaret River

During the 1990s, Xanadu enjoyed conspicuous success with its strong range of well-made wines. In 1999, the Lagan family sold out to a group of investors and by 2001 the company was listed on the stock exchange. With this financial boost, Xanadu has become a serious player, buying Normans Wines in 2002. Fortunately, quality has been maintained under long-time winemaker Jurg Muggli. The crisp but creamy Chardonnay and full-bodied Cabernet Sauvignon are among Margaret River's best. The Secession range is great value. ✎ *Boodjidup Rd, • 08 9757 2581 • www.xanaduwines.com* ☐ ▣ *red, white ★ Reserve Cabernet Sauvignon, Chardonnay, Secession Sauvignon Blanc-Semillon*

Margaret River Semillon

Think of Australian Semillon and the Hunter Valley in New South Wales immediately springs to mind. But the Margaret River region is also producing wines of the highest quality with this grape. Here, in a more temperate climate, Semillon is often rounder in flavor than in the Hunter Valley, acquiring more tropical fruit, yet maintaining its herbal edge. In cooler years, it has more in common with Sauvignon Blanc, offering grassy herbal notes and an edgy acidity. Producers, notably Moss Wood, who keep it as a varietal, make styles capable of ageing. Of more immediate appeal, however, is the region's signature Semillon-Sauvignon Blanc blend. Nowhere in Australia does it better: Margaret River "Semillon-Sauvignon" is vibrantly fruity with a generous palate. Producers like Cape Mentelle and Cullen even barrel-ferment some Sauvignon Blanc to give it increased complexity.

Picardy
Pemberton

After helping pioneer Cabernet Sauvignon at Moss Wood Winery *(see p100)* in Margaret River, Bill and Sandra Pannell sold out and moved on to establish Picardy in 1993. Their dream was to see how Chardonnay and Pinot Noir, as well as Shiraz and Cabernet Sauvignon, fared in the cooler Pemberton region. With the couple's interest in Burgundy, it was not the Pannells' minerally Chardonnay and racy Pinot Noir that made an impressive start. A deep-colored, spicy, rich Shiraz has also been produced. ✑ *Eastbrook Rd.*
• *08 9776 0036 • www.picardy.com.au*
◻ *by appt* 🔲 *red, white* ★ *Chardonnay, Pinot Noir, Shiraz*

Smithbrook Wines
Pemberton

This little-known company had large holdings planted in the late 1980s in the awakening Pemberton region and used to supply big name producers with grapes. However, a small amount was kept aside to make wine under the Smithbrook label, including a fresh and lively Sauvignon Blanc and a peachy Chardonnay. Bought by Brian Croser of Petaluma *(see p38)* in 1997, the label was revamped and, importantly, the company's Pinot Noir plantings were replaced by Merlot, which proved to be an inspired move. Soft, plummy, and—like all Smithbrook wines—great value, the Merlot is now viewed quite rightly as the flagship. ✑ *Smithbrook Rd. • 08 9772 3557 • www.smithbrook. com.au* ◻ *by appt* 🔲 *red, white*
★ *Merlot, Chardonnay, Sauvignon Blanc*

Alkoomi label

Chestnut Grove Wines
Manjimup

Chestnut Grove was established in 1991 with a range of gorgeous wines that helped put Manjimup on the map. Their passionfruit-infused Verdelho made the biggest noise, followed by a Merlot, weighty in alcohol and body, which belies Manjimup's reputation for being cool and marginal. But cool it definitely is, as shown in the Chestnut Grove Pinot Noir and Cabernet-Merlot. In 2002, the brand was bought by Australian Wine Holdings, but the founders, the Kordic family, still own the vineyard and winery.
✑ *Chestnut Grove Rd. • 08 9755 6046*
• *www.chestnutgrove.com.au* ◻
🔲 *red, white, sparkling* ★ *Verdelho, Semillon-Sauvignon Blanc, Merlot*

Stone Bridge Estate
Manjimup

Kate Hooker learned much of her winemaking trade in Champagne, Bordeaux, and Burgundy before coming home to the family winery. The experience was invaluable for dealing with the equally cool climate of Manjimup. Kate's strong suit is sparkling wine. Its full-flavored style is usually the result of at least 30 months on lees—a considerable investment for a small producer. ✑ *Holly's Rd. • 08 9773 1371*
◻ *by appt* 🔲 *red, white, sparkling*
★ *Pinot Noir-Chardonnay sparkling*

Alkoomi Wines
Great Southern

Riesling helped establish Alkoomi Wines and the Frankland area. The early Rieslings showed the kind of flavor intensity normally associated with the Clare or Eden valleys and

Western Australia—Producers

sparked immediate interest. Sea breezes help prolong the growing season, giving the grapes time to accumulate incredible richness. The climate seems to suit every variety that winemaker Merv Lange grows: Cabernet Sauvignon is deep in color and rich in fruit, and the black pepperiness of the Shiraz is also very appealing.
⊗ Wingebellup Rd., RMB 234, Frankland • 08 9855 2229 • www.alkoomiwines. com.au ⬜ 🖼 red, white ★ Shiraz, Cabernet Sauvignon, Riesling

Frankland Estate
Great Southern
Judi Cullam and Barrie Smith call one of their wines Isolation Ridge. And it is easy to see why: Frankland is one of the last pioneer wine regions in Australia. Cullam and Smith were farmers who moved into wine. They were apprenticed in France, and even managed to lure Bordeaux producer Jenny Dobson as an early winemaker. The restrained, elegant Bordeaux feel to their Cabernet Sauvignon makes it stand out in the Australian Cabernet crowd. The Shiraz can be vibrantly peppery, while the powerful Riesling has become an unofficial flagship.
⊗ Frankland Rd., Frankland • 08 9855 1544 • www. franklandestate.com.au ⬜ by appt 🖼 red, white ★ Riesling, Isolation Ridge Shiraz, Olmo's Reward (Bordeaux blend)

Plantagenet Wines
Great Southern
Plantagenet started life in an apple-packing shed in Mount Barker township in 1974, and established the area's early wine history. The locals considered the whole project madness, but bespectacled

Englishman Tony Smith persisted. First he made a fresh, aromatic Riesling, which looked and tasted unlike anything grown in Western Australia before. The Shiraz also wowed drinkers: all peppery and bouncy. As the fruit quality is so remarkably clean and fresh, Smith has pioneered an unoaked Chardonnay, too. ⊗ Albany Highway, Mount Barker • 08 9851 3111 • www.plantagenet wines.com ⬜ 🖼 red, white, dessert ★ Omrah: Shiraz, Unoaked Chardonnay, Mount Barker Cabernet Sauvignon

Wignalls Wines
Great Southern
Bill and Pat Wignall were thinking about growing Pinot Noir before many Australian drinkers had even heard of the grape. They believed that King River near Albany had much in common with Burgundy's Côte de Nuits and pressed forward with Pinot Noir, Chardonnay, and a little Cabernet Sauvignon. In 1998, the Wignalls spent one million dollars on a 400-ton winery and they now employ Ben Kagi, formerly of Rippon Vineyard, New Zealand, to oversee their Burgundian dream. ⊗ Chester Pass Rd., Albany • 08 9841 2848 • www. wignallswines.com ⬜ 🖼 red, white ★ Shiraz, Pinot Noir, Chardonnay

Best Western Australian Chardonnays

WINES OF NEW ZEALAND

Introducing New Zealand Wine

New Zealand's wine journey from total obscurity to international renown—especially for its Sauvignon Blanc and Pinot Noir—has taken place in the course of just 25 years. This was a formidable feat for a small country with a population of only four million, with little or no tradition of viticulture.

Early History

New Zealand's first vines were planted by English missionary Reverend Samuel Marsden in 1819 at Kerikeri on North Island. The first recorded wine was made in the 1830s in Waitangi by James Busby, the country's first resident British envoy. He was the man who had brought out a large number of European vines to Australia *(see p10)* and helped get Australia's wine industry started.

Leading grape variety Sauvignon Blanc

Busby did not have the same success with wine in New Zealand. The early years of British colonialism were taken up with wars and land disputes with the Maori, while the latter part of the 19th century saw gold rushes and the start of the refrigerated meat and dairy export trade that would dominate New Zealand's emerging agricultural economy.

There were, however, small corners of North Island where new immigrants were showing an interest in wine. In the late 1890s, Dalmatians (Slavs from present-day Croatia) started planting vineyards in Northland. The wine they made, chiefly for their own consumption, was often dismissed as "vile Austrian muck"—Croatia still being part of the Austro-Hungarian Empire. It came in for even more abuse during World War I.

After the war, many Dalmatians established small farms with vineyards in West Auckland. Here, the seeds were sown for the future explosion of the New Zealand wine industry by growers such as Ivan Yukich, who planted a vineyard called Montana in 1934, and Nikola Nobilo, who started his wine business in 1943. By the 1950s, most of the region's 80 vineyards were operated by families of Dalmatian descent, who formed a Viticulture Association to lobby government to deregulate the country's wine industry.

Montana's vineyards in Marlborough's Awatere Valley

 Preceding pages **Cloudy Bay vineyards in Wairau Valley, Marlborough**

Wine Regions

Vines are grown almost throughout the length of the country. Regions are very broadly defined, and often, especially in Canterbury and Waipara, the actual vineyards are clustered within small areas of the region. Key regions are Hawke's Bay and Wairarapa on North Island, Marlborough and Central Otago on South Island.

AUCKLAND & NORTHLAND
p114

36
Auckland

38
WAIKATO &
BAY OF PLENTY
p114

*North
Island*

GISBORNE
pp114–115

HAWKE'S BAY
pp115

*Tasman
Sea*

40

NELSON
p128

Wellington

WAIRARAPA
pp115

42

Nelson

MARLBOROUGH
p128

*Pacific
Ocean*

*South
Island*

Christchurch

44

CANTERBURY & WAIPARA
p129

46

Dunedin

CENTRAL OTAGO
p129

The Wine Revolution

The 1960s saw a fresh start with government backing for the industry and a sudden influx of international wine companies, including Penfolds, McWilliam's, and Seagram. With increased investment and enthusiasm came better viticulture, better grape varieties, and better wines.

Like Australia, New Zealand built its wine industry in the warmer northern regions where ripening could be assured: Auckland on North Island's west coast and Hawke's Bay on the east laid the early foundations. During the 1970s, however, the challenge was to see what South Island could do. Cooler sites were tried for the first time in Australia and New Zealand for varieties like Sauvignon Blanc, Chardonnay, Merlot, Cabernet Sauvignon, and Pinot Noir. New Zealand's biggest producer, Montana, is credited with planting the first vines in Marlborough in 1973. Its zesty 1980 Sauvignon Blanc was a revelation, and proved to be a catalyst for New Zealand's wine industry. It was responsible for stimulating the tastebuds of Australian winemaker, David Hohnen of Cape Mentelle *(see p98)*. After tasting a Marlborough Sauvignon, he traveled across the Tasman Sea to set up Cloudy Bay.

The first release here, by Kevin Judd in 1985, caused an international sensation. Other regions on the chilly South Island then opened up to vine-growing, including Nelson, Central Otago, and Canterbury. By 1990, there were 12,500 acres (5,000 ha) under vine. This was the start of a boom, which shows few signs of easing, with 39,000 acres (15,800 ha) of vineyards on the two islands combined.

Felton Road winery in Central Otago

The Wine Industry Today

New Zealand has become a quality player on the international wine scene. It currently boasts over 400 wineries. The industry crushed a record 118,000 tons of fruit in 2002, although this was a mere splash in the ocean compared with its big winemaking neighbor, Australia, which crushed an incredible 1.7 million tons in the same year.

The export market is definitely driving the boom times, having risen to a record level of NZ$246 million in 2002. Large companies are leading the way: Montana, which is now part of the huge international Pernod Ricard group, is the giant on the New Zealand wine scene with 35 percent of the total annual crush; Nobilo, bought up by Australian giant BRL Hardy in 2000, is in the number two spot; with Villa Maria, the country's largest privately owned winery, in third place. The heart and soul of New Zealand's wine industry remains in the many family-run wineries that dot the landscape. They may be small in size, but they make up the great majority of wineries and have been responsible for opening up whole new winegrowing regions such as Central Otago.

Grape Varieties and Wine Styles

The country's most popular variety is Sauvignon Blanc. It has now surpassed Chardonnay as the most widely planted grape, accounting for over 30 percent of the total vineyard area. Chardonnay, with 20 percent, is still holding its own and is capable of producing a wide range of styles. There is also a trend toward more red varieties. This has been led by the success of Pinot Noir, now the third most planted grape in the country with more than 7,400 acres (3,000 ha) under vine in 2004. The chances of producing vibrant varietal Pinot flavors increase on the cooler South Island, which is where the main growth has been. Merlot represents around eight percent of total plantings, and Riesling and Gewürztraminer are, despite fierce competition, gaining a foothold.

Yet the success of New Zealand wines, with their clear, crisp fruit flavors and freshness, has far from dulled the New Zealand wine growers' sense of exploration. The future of white varieties such as Pinot Gris looks very promising, and some makers are willing to explore territory that was once unthinkable—Syrah and Italian red varieties. There are still plenty more areas to be discovered and grape varieties to be tried.

Kameu River Wines, Auckland

 For more general information about wine, including styles, tasting terminology, and a glossary **See pp136–153**

Reading a New Zealand Wine Label

New Zealand wine labels are pretty straightforward. Many simply indicate just the producer, grape variety, and vintage. A system of "Certified Origin" was discussed in the 1990s, but no actual *guarantee of authenticity appears on the label. Wineries are, however, required to keep detailed records so that independent auditors can check the varieties of grapes used, their origins, and their vintage.*

Martinborough Vineyard is the name of the producer. This might, as in this case, be a small, independent producer or a big company that blends wines from vineyards right across the country.

Riesling is the grape variety, although by law, only 85 percent of the grapes used have to comply with what it says on the label.

Jackson Block is the name of the block of vines in the vineyard where the grapes were grown.

2002 indicates the vintage: the year in which the grapes were harvested.

The name and address of the producer is the main indication of the origin of this wine.

Estate bottled wine is usually the sign of a quality-conscious producer.

> Martinborough Vineyard
>
> RIESLING
>
> 2002
> JACKSON BLOCK
> No.07682
>
> PRODUCED AND ESTATE BOTTLED BY MARTINBOROUGH VINEYARD LTD.,
> PRINCESS STREET, MARTINBOROUGH, NEW ZEALAND.
> 12.5% VOL   PRODUCT OF NEW ZEALAND   750ml

Leading Grape Varieties

The three most widely grown varieties in New Zealand are the white grapes Sauvignon Blanc and Chardonnay, and the red grape Pinot Noir, all grapes whose original home was in the cooler-climate wine-producing regions of France.

Sauvignon Blanc
This Loire Valley grape is now the wine icon of New Zealand, especially the Marlborough region of South Island. It produces mainly fresh, zesty, herbal wines, but also examples that carry rich aromas and tropical fruit flavors.

Chardonnay
The world's most popular white grape is a native of Burgundy. In New Zealand, it can produce powerful, full-bodied wines, but most are less intensely flavored than their Australian and other New World counterparts.

Pinot Noir
The classic grape of red Burgundy is difficult to grow on foreign soil, as it needs time to ripen. Both Martinborough on North Island and Central Otago on South Island produce deep-colored wines with rich, creamy fruit that age well.

NEW ZEALAND–NORTH ISLAND

NORTH ISLAND

THIS IS THE MORE IMPORTANT *of the country's islands, where 70 percent of the population lives and where New Zealand's wine industry began. In New Zealand's recent wine boom, Marlborough on South Island may have attracted more attention, but North Island has started producing some fine wines, too, especially in the Hawke's Bay and Wairarapa areas.*

Although the big wine companies such as Montana and Nobilo have vast estates on South Island, they began life on North Island, and so have retained offices and wineries in Auckland. There are also many smaller producers experimenting with a wide range of grape varieties. Hawke's Bay on the central east coast is now producing consistently excellent Cabernet Sauvignon, and the region's Chardonnay and Sauvignon Blanc are equally praised. North of Hawke's Bay, at Gisborne, where the soil is more fertile but there is more cloud cover and rain, white grapes dominate, historically through large plantings of Müller-Thurgau

Key

North Island

but more recently with Chardonnay excelling. Further south, around Martinborough in the Wairarapa region, Pinot Noir is the star red, with some winemakers also producing fresh, crisp Chardonnays and Rieslings.

North Island's climate is fairly similar to that of Bordeaux, but with a much higher rainfall. The autumn period is rarely dry and, with the high humidity, growers often have trouble with rot at harvest time. Vintages vary from year to year and, with the wide variety of microclimates on the island, from region to region. However, most New Zealand winemakers have studied in Australia or Europe and are demonstrating increasing expertise in making quality wines.

View from the Goldwater Estate vineyards on Waiheke Island, Auckland

 Preceding pages **Newly-planted vineyard at the Craggy Range Winery, Martinborough, Wairarapa**

Regional Information at a Glance

Latitude 35–42°S.

Altitude 0–820 ft (0–250 m).

Topography Great variations, with mountains and volcanoes at the center and rivers flowing through terraced valleys. Vines are grown mainly in the coastal hills on the eastern side of the island.

Soil From fertile alluvial to infertile and sandy soil.

Climate Maritime. North Island is warmer and wetter than South Island and gets fewer hours of sunshine.

Temperature January (summer) average is 73°F (23°C).

Rainfall Annual average is 49 in (1,240 m). Heavy rains mean grapes are prone to damage and rot.

Wind Mainly westerly, with sea breezes.

Viticultural Hazards Phylloxera; leafroll viruses; fanleaf degeneration.

WINE AREAS & MAJOR PRODUCERS

Auckland & Northland *p114*

Babich Wines *p118*
Goldwater Estate *p118*
Kumeu River Wine *p118*
Montana Wines *p119*
Nobilo Wine Group *p119*
Stonyridge Vineyard *p120*
Villa Maria Estate *p120*

Waikato & Bay of Plenty *p114*

Gisborne *pp114–15*

Hawke's Bay *p115*

CJ Pask Winery *p120*
Corbans Winery *p121*
Craggy Range Winery *p121*
Te Mata Estate *p122*

Wairarapa *p115*

Ata Rangi *p122*
Dry River *p122*
Martinborough Vineyard *p122*
Palliser Estate *p123*

PACIFIC OCEAN

TASMAN SEA

Ahipara Bay
Kerikeri
Waitangi
AUCKLAND & NORTHLAND
Portland
Matakana
Hauraki Gulf
Waiheke Island
AUCKLAND
Kumeu
Manurewa
Lake Waikare
Kaimai Range
Waikato
Bay of Plenty
Hamilton
WAIKATO
Lake Taupo
BAY OF PLENTY
GISBORNE
Gisborne
Poverty Bay
HAWKE'S BAY
Napier
Hawke's Bay
Hastings
Wanganui
NORTH ISLAND
Otaki
Lake Wairarapa
WAIRARAPA
Martinborough
WELLINGTON
SOUTH ISLAND

35
36
37
38
39
40
41
42

Wine Areas of North Island

Auckland & Northland

This region is small in terms of the area of vines actually grown, but big in political power thanks to the huge number of wineries (90 in total). The country's top three producers—Montana, Nobilo, and Villa Maria—and most of the other major players, all have their headquarters in Auckland. Their wineries process grapes sourced both from inside the area and from all over New Zealand. Within the Auckland and Northland area there are seven smaller subregions producing contrasting wines: the newest, Matakana, is promising for reds, Waiheke Island, a short boat ride from Auckland, makes some of the best Cabernet Sauvignon-based wines, and Kumeu produces some exciting Chardonnay. *red-brown clays* 🍇 *Merlot, Cabernet Sauvignon* 🍇 *Chardonnay, Pinot Gris* 🍷 *red, white*

Waikato & Bay of Plenty

The beautiful adjoining wine areas of Waikato and Bay of Plenty are relative backwaters on the booming New Zealand wine

scene. However, this was not always the case: Waikato was the country's viticultural heart in the early 1900s thanks to the Te Kauwhata Viticultural Research Station. With just one percent of the country's vineyards, the area's glory days may now have passed. However, producers like Mills Reef, Rongopai, and Morton Estate still do the region proud, especially with their Chardonnays. The hotter, humid climate of Waikato also creates suitable conditions for producing botrytized dessert wines. 🍇 *free-draining brown-orange soils* 🍇 *Cabernet Sauvignon* 🍇 *Chardonnay, Sauvignon Blanc* 🍷 *red, white, dessert*

Villa Maria Estate Sauvignon Blanc

Gisborne

Gisborne, also known as Poverty Bay, is warm and sunny: ideal for creating well-rounded, friendly wines. It has carved a strong national reputation for its whites, Chardonnay and Gewürztraminer in particular. It is also one of the last areas in New Zealand to have significant plantings of the old—now generally considered passé—

Sheep grazing in a vineyard near Kumeu, Auckland and Northland

white favorite, Müller-Thurgau. This grape is often used, along with Muscat varieties, in cheap commercial brands. 🟫 gray-brown river silts 🍇 Chardonnay, Müller-Thurgau, Muscat varieties, Gewürztraminer, Riesling, Chenin Blanc 🍷 white

Hawke's Bay
Before Marlborough arrived on the scene in the mid-1970s, Hawke's Bay was New Zealand's principal viticultural region. The area has history (Te Mata is the site of the oldest New Zealand winery), suitable climate and soils, and pioneering spirit. Most wineries are located to the south around Hastings where the famous Gimblett Road gravels are found. The gravels, which had been laid down over millennia by the old Ngaruroro River, were exposed by catastrophic floods in 1867 and 1897. After the second flood, the river changed its course. Vine-growers here now have their own appellation "Gimblett Gravels." This generally warmer site produces some of the richest and ripest fruit in the region and is outstanding for its Cabernet Sauvignon and Merlot. Hawke's Bay is New Zealand's second

biggest growing region with over wine 50 producers. It is renowned for its rich Chardonnays and Cabernet Sauvignon blends, whose structure puts them in the Bordeaux league. 🟫 brown hill soils and river silts 🍇 Merlot, Cabernet Sauvignon 🍇 Chardonnay, Sauvignon Blanc 🍷 red, white

Wairarapa/Martinborough
Many people refer to Wararapa as Martinborough, because most of Wairapa's better-known vineyards are planted on the high alluvial terraces around the town of Martinborough. The soils here tend to be deep, free-draining gravels, which makes it ideal Pinot Noir territory. The Burgundy grape represents almost half of the plantings in the region, and is what originally put Wairarapa on the map. Climatically, the area is not unlike Marlborough on South Island with low rainfall, long hours of sunshine, and cool nights. The region is now a strong contender with its white varietals. Sauvignon Blanc and Chardonnay produced here can also be world class. 🟫 light gray-brown loess 🍇 Pinot Noir 🍇 Sauvignon Blanc, Chardonnay, Riesling 🍷 red, white

Vineyard in the Hawke's Bay area of North Island

Major Producers in North Island

Babich Wines
Auckland & Northland/ Marlborough
Babich has been a big name on the local wine scene since the family patriarch, Joe, founded the company in 1916. Long regarded as an industry stalwart—albeit a conservative one—Babich has been on a spending spree. In 1998, this winery invested in a 99-acre (40-ha) vineyard in Awatere Valley, Marlborough, followed by 160 acres (65 ha) in the nearby Waihopai Valley, as well as a quarter interest in Rapaura Vintners. The Patriarch and Mara (the family matriarch) brands do their namesakes proud, while the Irongate Chardonnay is one of the country's best. ⊛ *Babich Rd., Henderson • 09 833 7859 • www.babichwines.co.nz* 🔲 🎦 *red, white* ★ *Irongate Chardonnay, Patriarch Cabernet Sauvignon, Marlborough Sauvignon Blanc*

Goldwater Estate
Auckland & Northland/ Marlborough
An hour's ferry ride from Auckland lies the temperate and strongly maritime-influenced island of Waiheke, where some of New Zealand's best Cabernet Sauvignon can be found. The similarities between Waiheke Island and Bordeaux were lost on many until founder Kim Goldwater planted the first vines there in 1978. Goldwater Estate made its name with a Cabernet-Merlot blend, but more recently, the silky Esslin Merlot has grabbed drinkers' attention worldwide. ⊛ *18 Causeway Rd., Waiheke Island • 09 372 7493 • www.gold waterwine.com* 🔲 🎦 *red, white* ★ *Marlborough Chardonnay, Esslin Merlot, Cabernet Sauvignon-Merlot*

Kumeu River Wine
Auckland & Northland
New Zealand's first Master of Wine, Michael Brajkovich, is one of the country's premier Chardonnay makers; he seeks out the rich complexities in the grape that few

Maté's Vineyard, Kumeu River Wine

producers can match. In Maté's Vineyard Chardonnay, named after his late father, Brajkovich reaches the height of his craft. While Chardonnay is what the company is known for, its Pinot Gris, Pinot Noir, and Bordeaux red blends are also finely structured wines. After years of enduring cork taint as a necessary evil, Michael Brajkovich has taken the bold step of using screw caps across his entire range. ◈ *550 State Highway 16, Kumeu* • *09 412 8445* • *www.kumeuriver.co.nz* ◻ ▨ *red, white* ★ *Maté's Vineyard Chardonnay, Pinot Gris, Pinot Noir*

Montana Wines
Auckland & Northland/ Hawke's Bay/Marlborough
The company was started in 1944 by Croatian immigrant Ivan Yukich. New Zealand's biggest wine producer, Montana has its star performers, but also stays loyal to consumers of everyday drinking wines. In 2003, it crushed 50,000 tons of grapes, 35 percent of New Zealand's total production that year. The most arresting image of Montana Wines is of its Brancott Vineyard in Marlborough, nearly all its 730 acres (295 ha) devoted to one grape—Sauvignon Blanc. It was Montana's Sauvignon Blanc that first alerted the world to the great potential of this region. Montana also led the way with the first serious sparkling wine made in the country—the Marlborough Deutz Cuvée, made with input from the Champagne house Deutz. Montana's good relationship with producer Cordier is also contributing to considerable improvements in its reds. ◈ *333 Apirana Ave., Glen Innes* • *09 570 8400* • *www.montanawines.com* ◻ ▨ *red, white, sparkling, dessert* ★ *Marlborough Deutz Cuvée, Reserve Marlborough Chardonnay, Hawke's Bay Cabernet Sauvignon-Merlot*

The Rise & Rise of Pinot Noir
Twenty years ago, most New Zealand Pinot Noir was thin and rosé-like. Early clones of the Burgundy grape were unsuitable, many early sites more so. As viticulture improved, so did the wines. Martinborough on North Island led the way with wines deep in color and showing black cherry and savory aromas, and a distinct gaminess in taste. More than 40 percent of Pinot plantings are now found in Marlborough. Here, the grape is used in both sparkling and still wine production. Marlborough Pinot is the most approachable in style (and price), but for a Pinot with real bite, there are only two words you need to remember: Central Otago.

Nobilo Wine Group
Auckland & Northland/ Marlborough
Founded by Croatian immigrant Nikola Nobilo in 1943, Nobilo's early national prominence was built on the success of the aromatic white variety Müller-Thurgau. However, times have changed, and so has Nobilo. With an eye on popular tastes, it created White Cloud in the 1980s, an easy drinking Müller-Thurgau-Chenin Blanc blend produced in a distinctive misty bottle. It sold like hot cakes and inspired many copies—notably the Australian producer Seppelt Great Western's *(see p78)* Glass Mountain. BRL Hardy *(see p40)* took 100 percent ownership of Nobilo in 2000: a recent injection of capital has meant new planting programs in Marlborough and Hawke's Bay, making Nobilo the second largest wine producer in New Zealand. ◈ *45 Station Rd., Huapai* • *09 412 6666* • *www.nobilo.co.nz* ◻ ▨ *red, white, dessert* ★ *Icon Series Chardonnay, Icon Series Riesling, House of Nobilo Marlborough Sauvignon Blanc*

 Montana was bought by French drinks giant Pernod Ricard in 2005

Stonyridge Vineyard
Auckland & Northland

There is a distinctly Mediterranean feel at Stonyridge Vineyard. Founder Stephen White says it is in keeping with Waiheke's climate, which is around 4°F warmer than any other New Zealand wine region. White, a sailor-cum-surfer-cum-winemaker, was inspired to plant Bordeaux red grape varieties after working for Mas de Daumas Gassac in the South of France. Wine writers put Larose—a blend of five red varieties and one of the country's most expensive and in-demand wines—in the Bordeaux league. ⦿ *80 Onetangi Rd., Waiheke Island • 09 372 8822 • www.stonyridge.co.nz* ▢ 🍷 *red, white* ★ *Larose, Syrah*

CJ Pask Winery

Villa Maria Estate
Auckland & Northland/ Hawke's Bay/Marlborough

Founded in 1961, Villa Maria Estate is a wine giant, now third in New Zealand after Montana and Nobilo. The driving force is the hugely modest but determined owner, George Fistonich. His winemaking philosophy is focused on cheap and cheerful wines in keeping with the relative immaturity of the New Zealand wine industry. As the industry has grown, so too has Villa Maria Estate. The empire now embraces every price point and almost every major wine region. Of the five distinct ranges of wines, the Villa Maria Reserve label proudly leads the way. In 2005, a magnificent new winery and vineyard park were opened at the company's headquarters at Mangere. The site, landscaped to emphasize the spectacular natural amphitheater formed by the cone of an extinct volcano here, includes 50 acres (20 ha) of vineyard. ⦿ *118 Montgomerie Rd., Mangere, Auckland • 09 255 0660 • www.villamaria.co.nz* ▢ *by appt* 🍷 *red, white, sparkling, dessert* ★ *Reserve Wairau Valley Marlborough Sauvignon Blanc, Reserve Hawke's Bay Cabernet Sauvignon-Merlot, Reserve Hawke's Bay Noble Riesling*

CJ Pask Winery
Hawke's Bay

Chris Pask, a crop-spraying pilot, and Kate Radburnd, an award-winning winemaker, got together professionally in 1990 and have proved to be a great team ever since. Pask was the first person to recognize the potential of the

VINCENT GASNIER'S
TOP 10 New Zealand Wines for Storing

1. **Ata Rangi: Pinot Noir** (red) Wairarapa *p122*
2. **Cloudy Bay: Sauvignon Blanc** Marlborough *p130*
3. **Palliser Estate: Pinot Noir** Wairarapa *p123*
4. **Isabel Estate Vineyard: Sauvignon Blanc** Marlborough *p131*
5. **Pegasus Bay: Pinot Noir** Canterbury & Waipara *p132*
6. **Chard Farm: Pinot Noir** Central Otago *p132*
7. **Felton Road: Pinot Noir** (red) Central Otago *p133*
8. **Gibbston Valley Wines: Pinot Noir** Central Otago *p133*
9. **CJ Pask Winery: Cabernet Sauvignon-Merlot** Hawke's Bay *above*
10. **Kumeu River Wine: Chardonnay** Auckland & Northland *p118*

Corbans Winery vineyards

now famous Gimblett Road gravel soils and planted a range of both red and white varieties here. While pretty good at white winemaking, Radburnd's forte is red—her Merlot is one of the best in the country. Her Cabernet Sauvignon blend is consistent, and interest is high in what she will do with Syrah. ◎ *1133 Omahu Rd., Hastings • 06 879 7906 • www. cjpaskwinery.co.nz* ⬜ 🖼 *red, white* ★ *Reserve Merlot, Reserve Cabernet Sauvignon-Merlot, Reserve Chardonnay*

Corbans Winery
Hawke's Bay/Marlborough
Wine drinkers may well know Corbans through one or more of its many different guises: Longridge of Hawke's Bay, Stoneleigh Vineyard, Robard and Butler, Cook's Winemaker Reserve, International Cellars, and, of course, Corbans' own brand. Part of the huge Montana empire, Corbans has long been a major player in New Zealand's wine industry, even when it was still owned by the Corban family. Corbans delivers an extraordinary range of wines, from the economical White Label to the exclusive, flagship Cottage Block brand. These limited-edition wines are the product of specially

selected rows of vines that produce the very finest fruit. Cottage Block wines include a stonefruit-rich Chardonnay and, when conditions are favorable, a botrytized Noble Riesling. ◎ *91 Thames St., Napier • 06 833 6830 • www.adwnz.com* ⬜ 🖼 *red, white, sparkling, dessert* ★ *Cottage Block Chardonnay, Marlborough Sauvignon Blanc, Private Bin Noble Riesling*

Craggy Range Winery
Hawke's Bay/Wairarapa
Craggy Range was set up in 1998 by successful businessman Terry Peabody, who wanted to redirect his talents into making premium wines. Early releases suggest he is well on track. The project's linchpin is the progressive viticulturist and winemaker Steve Smith. A Master of Wine, Smith has planted vineyards in Martinborough and Hawke's Bay, including Syrah at the Gimblett Road site—an exciting addition to the region's red wine arsenal. Smith's belief in the importance of site selection is obvious from the name of the winery's restaurant: Terroir. ◎ *253 Waimarama Rd., Havelock North • 06 835 2011 • www.craggyrange. com* ⬜ 🖼 *red, white* ★ *Sauvignon Blanc, Chardonnay, Pinot Noir*

Te Mata Estate
Hawke's Bay

The first vines, Pinot Meunier, were planted here as early as 1892. Today, red is still the color that makes Te Mata one of the country's top producers. Cabernet Sauvignon, Merlot, and Cabernet Franc are the focus of owner John Buck's commitment to making wines of elegance and finesse. The top-of-the-range Coleraine Cabernet-Merlot blend and the much cheaper Awatea blend both enjoy a reputation for longevity, an elusive dream for some New Zealand red wine producers. Te Mata's long-time winemaker, Peter Cowley, has now moved into new, exciting territory with Syrah: his Bullnose Syrah virtually explodes with spice. 🌐 *Te Mata Rd., Havelock North • 06 877 4399 • www.temata.co.nz* 🔲 🖼 *red, white* ★ *Elston Chardonnay, Coleraine Cabernet Sauvignon-Merlot, Awatea Cabernet Sauvignon-Merlot, Bullnose Syrah*

Bullnose Syrah, Te Mata Estate

Ata Rangi
Wairarapa

The Maori phrase "Ata Rangi" translates as "new beginning" or "dawn sky"—fitting for a vineyard that helped to pioneer the modern era of winemaking in Martinborough. Founder Clive Paton bought a small plot here in 1980 and he and his wife, Phyllis, a former Montana winemaker, planted Burgundy varieties following a report by soil scientist Dr. Derek Milne that the region would be suited to them. By the 1990s, Ata Rangi was winning high esteem for its luxuriously big and silky Pinot Noir. 🌐 *Puruatanga Rd., Martinborough • 06 306 9570 • www.atarangi.co.nz* 🔲 🖼 *red, white, dessert* ★ *Pinot Noir, Craighall Chardonnay, Lismore, Pinot Gris*

Dry River
Wairarapa

In 2003, Dr. Neil McCallum stunned Dry River fans by selling his 20-acre (8-ha) vineyard to American buyers. However, the good news is that McCallum, the founder, inspiration, and winemaker, stayed on. He is considered a legend in Pinot Noir circles, and as a result, Dry River wines are some of the hardest to buy. His secret is obsessive attention to detail. Dry River shows the rich and complex side of the Pinot Noir grape. In fact, every grape McCallum touches should be tried. 🌐 *Puruatanga Rd., Martinborough • 06 306 9388* ⬛ 🖼 *red, white, dessert* ★ *Pinot Noir, Craighall Amaranth Riesling, Gewürztraminer*

Martinborough Vineyard
Wairarapa

It was Martinborough Vineyard that first put Martinborough on the map. Or was it the other way around? Whichever way it was, the winery is now responsible for some of

Vineyards in Martinborough, heart of the Wairarapa wine area

the most opulent Pinot Noir made in Australasia. Fruit ripeness is the key, something the company has worked hard on: great care has been taken over trellising and pruning techniques, as well as sourcing the best clones of grapes. Top results can also be seen in the powerful Chardonnay. During the 1990s, Martinborough was associated with winemaker Larry McKenna, a guru to the region's Pinotphiles. Now that he has left, the aim will be to maintain the high standard. So far? So good. ◐ *Princess St., Martinborough • 06 306 9955 • www.martinborough-vineyard.co.nz* ◻ ▣ *red, white* ★ *Reserve Pinot Noir, Chardonnay, Riesling*

Palliser Estate
Wairarapa
Like most of its fellow producers around Martinborough, Palliser made its name in the 1990s with Pinot Noir. Today, the company is an all-rounder with a selection of top-rung wines from Riesling to Chardonnay to Pinot Gris and Sauvignon Blanc. It even uses its Pinot Noir and Chardonnay grapes to make a *méthode champenoise* sparkling. Razor-sharp fruit intensity is the Palliser trademark. In fact,

the unwooded Sauvignon Blanc has such refreshing acidity and lasting flavors that it gives Marlborough a run for its money. With 210 acres (85 ha) under vine, Palliser is now one of the Martinborough region's largest wineries. ◐ *Kitchener St., Martinborough • 06 306 9019 • www.palliser.co.nz* ● ▣ *red, white, sparkling* ★ *Sauvignon Blanc, Riesling, Pinot Noir*

Other Producers in North Island

Mills Reef *(Hawke's Bay, Waikato & other areas)* 143 Moffat Rd., Tauranga • 07 576 8800 • www.millsreef.co.nz

Morton Estate Wines *(Hawke's Bay, Waikato, Marlborough & other areas)* Mountain Road, Epsom, Auckland • 09 300 5053 • www.mortonestatewines.co.nz

Rongopai *(Waikato)* Mountain Rd., Epsom, Auckland • 07 826 3462 • www.rongopaiwines.co.nz

Te Kairanga *(Wairarapa)* Martins Rd., Martinborough • 06 306 9122 • www.tkwine.co.nz

Vidal Estate *(Hawke's Bay & other areas)* 913 St. Aubyn St. East, Hastings • 06 876 8105 • www.vidal.co.nz

West Brook *(Auckland & Northland & other areas)* 215 Ararimu Valley Rd., Waimauku • 09 411 9924 • www.westbrook.co.nz

NEW ZEALAND–SOUTH ISLAND

SOUTH ISLAND

SOUTH ISLAND HAD VIRTUALLY NO WINE INDUSTRY *to speak of until the early 1970s when Montana Wines planted the first vines in the Marlborough region. The success they enjoyed with Sauvignon Blanc sent wine prospectors in search of other cool-climate growing areas. Central Otago, in the far south of the island, proved ideally suited to Pinot Noir.*

If there is one grape variety that has become synonymous with New Zealand, it is Sauvignon Blanc, and Sauvignon Blanc from Marlborough is the most famous. Situated at the northern tip of South Island, Marlborough has a gravel soil and dry, sunny climate that suits Chardonnay as well as Sauvignon Blanc and with potential too for Cabernet Sauvignon. The high acidity of the white grapes also makes them ideal for sparkling wine.

Just west of Marlborough and, almost literally, in its shadow in terms of fame if not quality, the region of Nelson is known as the sunniest place in New Zealand. Recent grubbing up of apple orchards has left land free for vineyards, and Nelson Sauvignon Blanc could well be one of the star wines of the future.

In general, the climate of South Island is noticeably cooler than that of North Island, but with more hours of sunshine and less rainfall. Central Otago can boast that it is the most southerly winemaking region in the world. Many people thought temperatures there would surely be too low for anything but white grapes. All the more astonishing then that Pinot Noir should have become the flagship wine from this area and winemakers are flocking to buy land here, making this the fastest-growing wine region in New Zealand.

Key

South Island

Rippon Vineyard beside Lake Wanaka, Central Otago

 Preceding pages **Vineyard in the Wairau Valley, Marlborough**

WINE AREAS & MAJOR PRODUCERS

Regional Information at a Glance

Latitude 41–46°S.

Altitude 33–1,310 ft (10–400 m). The highest vineyards are those in the Central Otago region.

Topography Dramatic variations, with high mountains and deep valleys running out to broad plains. Vines are mainly grown on flat or gently sloping land.

Soil From fertile alluvial to infertile and sandy soil.

Climate South Island is cooler but drier than North Island. Marginal sites, frosts, and scarcity of water make viticulture more problematic here.

Temperature January (summer) average is 64°F (18°C).

Rainfall Annual average is 32 in (810 mm).

Wind Mainly westerly. Prevailing winds come from the Southern Alps.

Viticultural Hazards Phylloxera; fanleaf degeneration; leafroll viruses.

Wither Hills Sauvignon Blanc

Wine Areas of South Island

Nelson

The Nelson region has a number of things in common with its more famous neighbor, Marlborough. It is warm and sunny, but autumn rains can often hinder ripening. Hermann Seifried planted his first vines here in 1974, and the Seifried Estate is still the region's biggest producer. Nelson falls into two distinct climate and soil areas: the river silt flats of the Waimea Plains and the higher reaches of the Upper Moutere Hills.

Sauvignon Blanc from Cloudy Bay

 yellow-gray stony silts (river), clay loam (hills)  Pinot Noir, Cabernet Sauvignon 🅱 Chardonnay, Sauvignon Blanc, Riesling 🔴 red, white

---

Sauvignon Blanc from Marlborough

Drinking Marlborough Sauvignon Blanc has been likened to jumping naked into a gooseberry bush. It is an exhilarating wine rush. The area's first Sauvignon Blanc, from Montana Wines, caused a stir in 1973 with its cut-grass pungency. It was seen as uniquely New Zealand, unable to be replicated elsewhere, not even in the grape's native French region, the Loire. Marlborough has a number of things that sit right with Sauvignon: plenty of sunshine and a long growing season that ensures grapes ripen fully. Soil type is important, too: the region's fertile, silty soils produce a zingy style of Sauvignon, while the stony sites, where the heat is trapped during the day and released at night, result in a less aggressive wine. Virtually all Marlborough's wineries now produce Sauvignon Blanc, but styles differ: some are fiercely herbal, others ripe and tropical.

Marlborough

From a standing start in 1973, Marlborough has raced ahead to become New Zealand's premier wine region. It now boasts over 40 percent of all the country's vineyards. Among its many attractions are a long, slow ripening season, masses of sunshine, cool nights, and low rainfall. Little wonder it has far more wineries (around 70) than any other South Island region. Despite these advantages, Marlborough is not the perfect area for growing vines. Frosts and lack of water for irrigation, especially in the arid hill regions, are a constant problem.

The wine region centers on the plains of the Wairau Valley, a long valley flanked by mountains opening out into the wide, shallow Cloudy Bay. Glacial outwash has formed wide terraces of silt and stones. During the day, the stones absorb heat, which is then emitted again at night; they also provide good drainage. With the Wairau Valley now carpeted with vines, the price of land has rocketed, and other valleys are attracting growers, notably the Awatere Valley to the south.

Early expansion in Marlborough was due to one grape variety—Sauvignon Blanc—responsible for the runaway success story of Cloudy Bay (see p130). In the 1980s, the region also began to deliver the nation's best sparkling wines and proved it was suitable for growing Pinot Noir and Chardonnay, too. 🌾 stony, yellow-gray river silts 🍷 Pinot Noir 🍇 Riesling, Gewürztraminer, Sauvignon Blanc, Chardonnay, 🔴 red, white, sparkling

The dramatic landscape of South Island

Canterbury & Waipara

With its proximity to the Southern Alps, little wonder this region used to be considered too cold for grapes. It is borderline for some varieties, but not for Pinot Noir and Chardonnay—especially in Waipara, which is located on the Canterbury Plains, protected by the lush Teviotdale Hills around Pegasus Bay. 🖾 gray alluviums, stony yellow-gray sediments 🖾 Pinot Noir 🖾 Chardonnay, Riesling, Sauvignon Blanc 🖾 red, white

Central Otago

This winter playground lies in the rain shadow of the Southern Alps, where vines often have to be planted on hillsides to maximize sunshine and escape frosts. It is the world's most southerly wine region and one of the last to fall to the vine—the first wines were not produced here until the 1980s. Now it is catching up fast, and in terms of the area

under vine, it is New Zealand's fourth largest region, after Marlborough, Hawke's Bay, and Gisborne. Its reputation rests largely on the extraordinary success of Pinot Noir, although growers have also had good results with Chardonnay, Pinot Gris, and Riesling. The continental climate produces wines of elegance and finesse, but the winemaking costs in Central Otago's difficult climate and terrain are the highest in the country. 🖾 yellow-brown from alpine terrain 🖾 Pinot Noir 🖾 Chardonnay, Pinot Gris, Riesling 🖾 red, white

VINCENT GASNIER'S TOP 10 Outstanding New Zealand Sauvignon Blancs

1. **Cloudy Bay**
   Marlborough p130
2. **Isabel Estate Vineyard**
   Marlborough p131
3. **Huia Vineyards**
   Marlborough p130
4. **West Brook: Blue Ridge** Hawke's Bay, Marlborough p123
5. **Palliser Estate**
   Wairarapa p123
6. **Neudorf Vineyards**
   Nelson p130
7. **Craggy Range Winery**
   Hawke's Bay p121
8. **Wither Hills Vineyards**
   Marlborough p132
9. **Dry River**
   Wairarapa p122
10. **Villa Maria Estate**
    Auckland & Northland, Marlborough p120

A Frenchman named Feraud planted a vineyard in Central Otago in 1864 at the time of the gold rush, some 120 years before anyone else

The spectacular setting of Lake Wanaka in Central Otago

Major Producers in South Island

Neudorf Vineyards
Nelson

Nelson has something its superstar neighbor, Marlborough, does not: Neudorf Vineyards. In this tiny vineyard belonging to the Finn family, lies a fully-fledged, red-hot Chardonnay of international repute: the Cloudy Bay of New Zealand Chardonnays. Immensely approachable, combining flavor-rich power and elegance, Neudorf is consistently rated as one of New Zealand's greatest versions of this grape. Tim Finn approaches his task like an architect—structure is everything. His eye for detail applies equally to his highly regarded Pinot Noir. ◈ *Neudorf Rd., Upper Moutere • 03 543 2643 • www.neudorf.co.nz* ☐ ▨ *red, white* ★ *Moutere Chardonnay, Sauvignon Blanc, Moutere Reserve Pinot Noir*

Cloudy Bay
Marlborough

The bay where Marlborough's Wairau River flows into the sea was named "Cloudy" by Captain Cook when he was charting the coast of New Zealand in 1770. The Marlborough winery that took the name when it was founded in 1985 has brought it lasting fame. Cloudy Bay defined the archetypal New Zealand Sauvignon Blanc and became an international celebrity. Fruit sweetness countered with tangy gooseberries set the benchmark, and in warm years, a splash of Semillon did wonders. Winemaker Kevin Judd's style has been copied across New Zealand and Australia, but it still sets the pace. A world-class sparkling, Pelorus, was released in 1992. But that is not all. The Cloudy Bay portfolio is full of great wines: classy Chardonnay, Pinot Noir, an avant-garde wooded Sauvignon Blanc, Te Koko, a late-harvested Riesling, and a stunning Gewürztraminer. There is virtually nothing Cloudy Bay does not do well. Of course, it helps being part of the giant Louis Vuitton Moët Hennessy group. ◈ *Jacksons Rd., Blenheim • 03 520 9140 • www.cloudybay.co.nz* ☐ ▨ *red, white, sparkling, dessert* ★ *Pelorus Vintage Sparkling, Sauvignon Blanc, Pinot Noir*

Huia Vineyards
Marlborough

A bottle of Cloudy Bay Sauvignon Blanc tasted in 1989 was career defining for Claire and Mike Allan. The wine's explosive flavors convinced the couple, studying winemaking in Australia, to head to Marlborough. They set up Huia (pronounced who-ya) Vineyards in 1996 and proceeded to create some of the most spine-tingling Sauvignon Blancs in the region. Their hallmark is a firm structure with a bone-dry finish. The Allans have now followed up with a fabulous sparkling wine, Huia Brut, and a range of fine aromatic whites—Riesling, Pinot Gris, and a luscious, spicy Gewürztraminer. The name Huia honors a New Zealand bird that was hunted to extinction for the sake of its striking white-tipped, black tail-feathers in the early years of the 20th century. ✎ Boyces Rd., RD3, Blenheim • 03 572 8326 • www.huia.net.nz ☐ 🖥 red, white, sparkling ★ Huia Brut, Sauvignon Blanc, Riesling, Gewürztraminer

Isabel Estate Vineyard
Marlborough
We can thank the late Isabel Tiller for the wines from this exciting Marlborough vineyard. She planted the first vines here in 1982 and encouraged her son Michael to take up grape-growing. Everything has been planned, slow and steady, with the Tillers (Michael and wife Robyn) first growing grapes for other producers before establishing a winery of their own in 1997. Their wines, each an expression of the estate's *terroir*, are noted for their great flavor concentration and persistence in the mouth. Quality is outstanding across the range. ✎ 72 Hawkesbury Rd., Renwick • 03 572 8300 • www.isabelestate.com ☐ 🖥 red, white, dessert ★ Sauvignon Blanc, Riesling, Noble Sauvage (botrytis white: Sauvignon Blanc or Riesling depending on year)

Jackson Estate
Marlborough
John Stichbury's family was farming the Jackson Estate in the Wairau Valley back in the mid-19th century, nearly 150 years before anyone thought of planting the area with Sauvignon Blanc. Where his great-grandfather, Adam Jackson, grew wheat and barley, John now produces some of New Zealand's best Sauvignon Blanc. Other varieties, including Riesling, Chardonnay, and Pinot Noir, are grown, but Sauvignon Blanc accounts for three-quarters of the annual crush. The new premium Grey Ghost version, released in 2005, has a little more body and hints of vanilla from its ageing in oak, but it is the standard Jackson Estate Sauvignon Blanc that continues to be the company's flagship wine. Bursting with gooseberry and tropical fruit, it is excellent value for money. Ever since its first vintage in 1991, it has shown a consistency that is the envy of other growers. ✎ 22 Liverpool Street, Riverlands • 03 579 5523 • www.jacksonestate.co.nz ☐ by appt 🖥 red, white ★ Sauvignon Blanc

Huia Vineyards, one of the many successful new wineries in the Marlborough

Wither Hills Vineyards
Marlborough

This used to be a successful, smallish player on the New Zealand wine scene, run by its founder, the charismatic Brent Marris. His father, John, had been one of the first to plant contract-grown grapes in the Marlborough region, back in 1978. Father and son merged their holdings in 1999 to give the company a total of some 740 acres (300 ha) of prime vineyards in the Wairau Valley. Enter beer and drinks giant Lion Nathan in 2002 with some NZ$52 million, and Wither Hills became part of this growing Australasian empire. Questions were asked about the future of Brent Marris, but so far, it is business as usual. Marris has a talent for being financially astute as well as a good winemaker. He concentrates on just three wines—Sauvignon Blanc, Chardonnay, and Pinot Noir—and achieves a highly

PRIMA DONNA

Pegasus Bay wine label

consistent standard that never drops below outstanding. ⓢ *114 New Renwick Rd., RD2, Blenheim • 03 578 4036 • www.witherhills. co.nz* ◻ 🔲 *red, white* ★ *Sauvignon Blanc, Chardonnay, Pinot Noir*

Pegasus Bay
Canterbury & Waipara

Ivan Donaldson, an associate professor of neurology as well as a winemaker, certainly has an enquiring mind, which in Pegasus Bay's formative years was responsible for pursuing not just fruit flavor, but complexity and texture. A family enterprise, Pegasus makes strong statements with its wines. Whether it is the Sauvignon Blanc-Semillon, Riesling, Chardonnay, or Pinot Noir, flavors are rich and dramatic—in keeping with the Donaldsons' love of opera (and operatic wine names, such as their late-picked Riesling, Aria, and their unfiltered Pinot Noir, Prima Donna). ⓢ *Stockgrove Rd., Amberley • 03 314 6869 • www.pegasusbay.com* ◻ 🔲 *red, white* ★ *Sauvignon Blanc-Semillon, Chardonnay, Prima Donna Pinot Noir*

Chard Farm
Central Otago

Bungee-jumping originated in the gorges near Chard Farm, which gives some idea of the dramatic local landscape. The winery was started in 1987 by brothers Rob and Greg Hay, and this cool site is perfect for aromatic Riesling, as well as Burgundy soul mates Chardonnay and Pinot Noir. Ripening can be a problem, so Rob (Greg left in 1998) chaptalizes (adds sugar) to boost alcoholic strength. The Riesling is stunning, but the Chardonnay and Pinot Noir fight it out for flagship honors. Hay

Brent Marris: Winemaker Extraordinaire

With a high charm factor, and a faultless winemaking resumé, Brent Marris is a pin-up of the New Zealand wine industry. Marlborough's first qualified winemaker, Marris started up Wither Hills Vineyards in 1994. The impact of his exceptional Chardonnay was almost instant. Success followed with a multi award-winning Sauvignon Blanc and now with Pinot Noir. As a senior wine judge on the Australian and New Zealand show circuit, Marris knows what people want: strong, clean fruit flavors, classy, understated oak input, and layered, elegant complexity.

makes a number of styles of each variety: Judge and Jury Chardonnay and Finla Mor Pinot Noir reach heady climaxes.
Ⓢ *Gibbston, RD1, Queenstown* • *03 442 6110* • *www.chardfarm.co.nz* ▢ 🔖 *red, white* ★ *Riesling, Judge and Jury Chardonnay, Finla Mor Pinot Noir*

Felton Road
Central Otago
Felton Road is to the Central Otago region what Cloudy Bay was to Marlborough in the 1980s. Planted in 1991, the first releases of Pinot Noir here startled tastebuds with an energized fruit intensity. Central Otago Pinot Noir, and Felton Road in particular, became hot property. The wine developed a legion of fans, especially in the UK from where owner Nigel Greening hails. He believes that Central Otago's fruit quality is due to a huge difference in temperatures between night and day: from 37° to 91°F (3° to 33°C). Viticulture here is largely organic, while the winemaking is minimalist and focused on Old-World techniques. The wines are strongly individual, showing exceptionally bright, pristine fruit. Ⓢ *Bannockburn, RD2* • *03 445 0885* • *www.feltonroad.com* ▢ 🔖 *red, white, dessert* ★ *Block 5 Pinot Noir, Dry Riesling, Barrel-Fermented Chardonnay*

Gibbston Valley Wines
Central Otago
As well as the twin attractions of skiing and bungee jumping, there is now another reason to visit Queenstown: the wine. From being unheard of 15 years ago, Gibbston Valley Wines has become a leading Pinot Noir maker in Central Otago. The climate here is cool and marginal for grapes, so the expertise of Otago-born, Napa Valley-trained

winemaker Grant Taylor is vital. Expect wines of great vibrancy and purity of fruit. Gibbston Valley does well with the aromatic white variety Pinot Gris, which could ultimately prove the best white grape for the region. Pinot Noir is supple and one of the more full-blooded wines made here: its reserve is the flagship.
Ⓢ *Queenstown-Cromwell Hwy, Gibbston* • *03 442 6910* • *www.gvwines.co.nz* ▢ 🔖 *red, white, dessert* ★ *Riesling, Chardonnay, Reserve Pinot Noir*

Rippon Vineyard
Central Otago
Rippon Vineyard is breathtakingly beautiful with its shimmering blue Lake Wanaka, and the snow-capped Buchanan Range backdrop. With an undisputed pristine, alpine-fresh fruit quality, the wines are as awe-inspiring as the view. Of course, when the first plot of some 30 varieties was planted at Rippon in 1974, there was a great sense of the unknown. Ten years later, after making experimental batches, choices were made. Pinot Noir it was, as well as some whites. Ⓢ *Mount Aspiring Rd., Lake Wanaka* • *03 443 8084* • *www.rippon. co.nz* ▢ 🔖 *red, white, sparkling* ★ *Pinot Noir, Riesling, Gewürztraminer*

Other Producers of South Island

Lawson's Dry Hills (Marlborough)
Alabama Road, Blenheim • *03 578 7674* • *www.lawsonsdryhills.co.nz*

Nautilus Estate (Marlborough)
12 Rapaura Rd., Renwick • *03 572 9364* • *www.nautilusestate.com*

Peregrine Wines *Kawarau Gorge Rd., Queenstown* • *03 442 4000* • *www.peregrinewines.co.nz*

Seifried (Nelson) *Redwood Rd., Appleby* • *03 544 5599* • *www.seifried.co.nz*

Vavasour (Marlborough)
Redwood Pass Road, Seddon • *03 575 7481* • *www.vavasour.com*

Thanks to the proximity of some of the country's best mountain resorts, wine tourism is a thriving industry in Central Otago

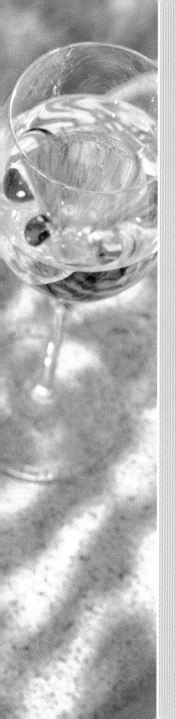

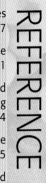

REFERENCE

Wine Styles

Obviously, no two wines are ever exactly alike, but wine styles (excluding fortified wines such as port and sherry) can be broadly divided into the ten categories set out below. Examples from Australia and/or New Zealand are given for each style.

Sparkling

Sparkling wines run the gamut from light-as-air Italian prosecco to elegant, steely French Champagnes that mellow with age, to rich, heart-warming, toasty bubblies from warmer New World vineyards and ripe-fruit red sparkling Shiraz from Australia. The classic blend for sparkling wine (Champagne in particular) is Chardonnay, Pinot Noir, and Pinot Meunier. This combination develops fruitiness with firmness and fragrance. Top sparkling wines also gain complexity from the second fermentation in bottle and contact with the finished fermentation yeasts. Good Champagne should have complex toast, nut, butter, and cookie flavors, and the bubbles should give a tingling sensation to balance the flavor.
★ *"Traditional method" sparkling wines from Australia and New Zealand, Sparkling Shiraz from Victoria*

Crisp, dry, light-bodied whites

Expect pale, white, even green-tinged colors in the glass, and green apple, fresh-mown grass, wet stones, and sometimes gooseberry on the nose. These wines will be light, with neutral aromas backed up by crisp acidity and tangy, refreshing fruit on the palate—with flavors of apples, pears, citrus fruits. Grapes to watch out for are Pinot Blanc, Pinot Gris, Sauvignon Blanc, Riesling, and lighter versions of Chardonnay. These wines are not widely found in the New World (except the coolest parts of New Zealand); classic examples from the Old World include Vinho Verde from Portugal and Chablis and Muscadet from France. Oak-ageing does a crisp, dry white no favors; it should be refreshing on the palate and is best drunk young.
★ *New Zealand Riesling, Chardonnay, and Pinot Gris*

Aromatic or flowery, dry to medium-sweet whites

Aromatic wines may have a strong color, but it is on the nose that they really make their mark. Expect anything from honey and hay (Riesling), to smoky citrus notes (Pinot Gris), peaches (Viognier), to pure grape flavors (Muscat) and even roses, lychees, and Turkish delight from the most aromatic grape of all, Gewürztraminer. Most of these aromas will be backed up on the palate with similar flavors, but wines can vary from light and delicate (Germany, Greece) to robustly perfumed and weighty (Alsace, Australia).

The powerful aromatic character of these wines can integrate well with a touch of sugar, so some are made in an "off-dry" or medium-sweet style. No sensible producer will smother the lively character with oak.
★ *Gewürztraminer, Australian Riesling*

Tangy or steely, medium-bodied whites

Less flamboyant on the nose, but more assertive on the palate than aromatic wines, tangy/steely styles are some of the best to pair with food. Expect creamier, smoother aromas and allow time for these to open out in the glass as the wine warms up, and as it ages. Firm-fruited flavors tend to mellow as the wine gets older. Tangy wines suggest hazelnuts (Chardonnay), damp stones (Chenin Blanc), and beeswax (Semillon); steely ones lean toward flint and gooseberries (Sauvignon Blanc), and limes (Riesling). In general, tangy wines respond better to oak-ageing than steely ones, but not for long: the strong vanilla flavors of oak can easily overpower them.
★ *Sauvignon Blanc from Marlborough, Nelson, and Wairarapa (New Zealand) and Adelaide Hills (South Australia), Australian Riesling, Western Australian Semillon-Sauvignon Blanc, Hunter Valley Semillon*

Full-bodied, rich flavored whites

Full-on, bold, and golden in the glass, these wines look as luscious as they taste. Expect a waft of buttery, honeyed aromas, along with tropical fruit, peaches, nectarines, even pineapple. There will be a similar barrage of rich, mouth-filling flavor on the palate. Full-bodied whites often have higher alcohol, but the best of them still have a twang of acidity to keep them balanced.

They all benefit from additional vanilla oak characters, but should not be overwhelmed by them. Many gain complexity with age. Full-bodied whites hail mainly from warmer New World countries, but pockets of the Northern Rhône, Languedoc-Roussillon, and central Spain also produce powerful whites.

★ *Australian Chardonnay*

Rosé

Made from red grapes, but left only for a limited time with the color-giving grape skins, rosé can vary from palest powderpuff pink (California Zinfandel), to deep opaque red (Australian Grenache), depending on how long the grapes macerate. Many have the weight of a white wine on the palate, but the aromas of red fruits and hedgerow berries nearly always give away their red grape origins. Lighter wines—generally from Old World countries (Loire Valley and Provence in France, Navarra in Spain)—will be delicate, thirst-quenching, and tangy with a hint of red fruits. Heavier ones—from the Rhône Valley and Australia—have richer, deeper, almost red wine flavors, sometimes with a touch of tannin.

★ *Australian Grenache*

Fresh, fruity, low tannin reds

This style is red wine at its simplest, freshest, and most juicy. These pinky reds are for drinking as young as possible, as they will greet you with pure, primary fruit aromas of raspberry, red apple, and cherry, backed up with cheery red-fruit characters that fill the palate. There will be no chalky tannins getting in the way of their

satiny smoothness, and any acidity will be soft and supple. Fresh, fruity reds are as likely to come from the Old World as the New, from grapes low in tannin, such as Gamay, Grenache, and Barbera. In hotter countries where grapes get riper in the sun, tannins are often overtaken by full, fruity flavors, so a usually robust grape like Merlot can exchange its tannin for plummy fruit. These reds trade on their fruity freshness, so are best without ageing in oak.

★ *Australian Grenache, lighter Merlots (Australia and New Zealand)*

Medium to full-bodied reds

This group includes the world's classic red wines, which first and foremost have a firm structure and plenty of backbone. In medium- to full-bodied Old World wines—such as Burgundy, Bordeaux and Barolo—aromas and flavors might not be very expressive at first, but with a year or two's age, the wines will open up to reveal wafts of bramble fruit, mulberry, plum, and violet. They develop in a similar way on the palate too: youthful hard tannins will soften, and as the wines mature, their range of fruit flavors will evolve to include cranberries, spice, truffles, and chocolate. Medium- and full-bodied reds call out for oak, which adds both structure and a touch of vanilla aroma. These wines match perfectly with meat dishes.

★ *Pinot Noir from Central Otago and Wairarapa (New Zealand) and Yarra Valley (Australia), Cabernet Sauvignon-Merlot blends (Australia and Hawke's Bay, New Zealand)*

Full, powerful, often spicy reds

These are the most mouth-filling wines of all. Grapes such as Cabernet Sauvignon (blackcurrant), Shiraz (spicy plum and liquorice), and Zinfandel (leather and strawberries) dominate this category. The wines are a rich, inky color in the glass, show intense, sweet, dark fruit on the nose, then dense, velvety-smooth fruit on the palate. These wines are mainly from grapes tough enough to survive in the hot vineyards of the New World or the Rhône Valley. Many will develop in the cellar, but their overwhelming ripeness also makes them fruity enough to drink young. They all need oak to balance their powerful fruit flavors.

★ *Australian Shiraz and Mourvèdre, Cabernet Sauvignon (South Australia, New South Wales and Margaret River)*

Sweet/Dessert

Sweet wines vary from light, delicate, grapey versions from the Muscat grape to full-on Australian liqueur wines (again Muscats), which display all the golden sunshine of their origins. The former are aperitifs, the latter dessert wines, too, concentrated for drinking with a meal. In between are a host of sweet wines with richly honeyed aromas and buttery-smooth flavors. All sweet wines should have a crisp acidity to balance the sweetness of their fruit or they become lifeless. Sweet wines made from the Riesling grape are some of the zestiest.

★ *Botrytized and late-harvest sweet wines from Riverina, New South Wales, Liqueur Muscat (Australia)*

For details on the practicalities of winetasting and a glossary of common terms used to describe wine **See pp138–141**

Tasting Wine

Wine can simply be consumed like any other beverage. Tasting wine, however, entails a more thoughtful, methodical approach. The following notes are designed to help you to maximize the pleasure you derive from every glass.

Practicalities

It is best to taste wine in a naturally lit, odorless room to allow its true color to be examined and to avoid other aromas interfering with the sense of smell. Avoid perfume, mints, and smoke. The most important factor when tasting is the shape and size of glass, as this can have a major impact on the taste of a wine *(See p146).*

Look

Looking at a wine can provide valuable clues to its character. Note the color and check that the wine is clear—cloudiness can indicate a fault. For reds, tilt the glass away from you against a white background and inspect the rim of the liquid to see the true color. As a red wine ages, it changes from bright purple to tawny and then to brown. So if a red wine looks brown, it may be past its best (although brown would be normal in wines such as sherry and tawny port). A deep golden color in a white wine may indicate the wine has been aged in oak, but it can also indicate a sweet wine style or particularly ripe fruit.

Smell

Smelling wine will vastly improve your enjoyment and knowledge. Firstly, gently sniff the wine. Make a note of any first impressions, as they are often the most revealing.

Holding the glass by its stem, swirl the wine in order to help release its aromas. Then take another sniff. Note the fruit aromas you detect now. Are they intense, or relatively subdued? Is there a range of suggested "flavors?" If so, this might indicate complexity, a sign of quality. Does it smell of the fruity flavors often found in a young wine, or does it boast more mature, developed aromas such as mushrooms, leather, and diesel? Is any one smell dominant, and do you like it? *See pp140–141* for help in identifying some of the aromas you may detect.

Taste

This stage often merely confirms the impression received on the nose. Take a small sip and allow the wine to linger on your tongue and mouth. You can enhance the flavors by pursing your lips and sucking a small amount of air into your mouth. This takes practice, but it is something professional tasters encourage as the presence of oxygen amplifies the flavors experienced. If you are tasting a lot of wines in one session, it is normally sensible to spit out each wine after noting the flavors and neutralize the palate by eating a cracker or taking a sip of water. Here are some further guidelines:

• Note the sweetness of the wine, detected on the tip of the tongue. Is it dry, medium, or sweet?

• Consider the acidity— the element of a wine that keeps it fresh—detected on the sides of the tongue. Is it in balance with the rest of the wine?

• How heavy does the wine feel in your mouth? Do you think it is light-, medium-, or full-bodied?

• Assess the wine's fruit qualities. Are they pure and fruity (as in a young wine), or mature and complex (as in an older one)?

• Can you recognize any individual flavors?

• With red wines, think about tannins—the drying, mouth-puckering elements picked up by your gums. Are they harsh and bitter, or in balance with the wine?

Finish

Consider how long the flavors last in your mouth after you spit or swallow. This is known as the "finish" and, in general, the longer it lasts, the better the wine.

Describing a Wine

It is virtually impossible to express in words the complexities and subtleties of even the most basic of wines. When it comes to identifying aromas and flavors, wine tasters borrow their vocabulary from all kinds of areas, including fruits, flowers, spices, nuts, and types of wood. Some of the flavor compounds actually exist in certain wines. For example, vanilla aromas come from vanillin, which occurs naturally in new oak barrels. However, others are mere impressions that wines create in the mind of the taster. Everyone's sense of smell and taste is, of course, different, as we all have our own memory bank of flavors.

Descriptive Terms

There are a large number of commonly used words and phrases for discussing the style and character of a wine. Definitions are not water-tight and there is often a large margin of overlap between the various terms.

age-worthy Applied to wines that will benefit from further maturation in the bottle. Typical examples of age-worthy wines are young with either powerful tannins, good acidity, or some sweetness.

aromatic A wine with lots of perfumed, fruity aromas, which normally leap out of the glass. Aromatic grape varieties include Sauvignon Blanc, Riesling, Gewürztraminer, and Muscat.

austere A wine that lacks fruity flavors and displays harsh, bitter tannins and/or high acidity.

acidic All wines need acidity to keep them balanced, but too much is a fault. Acidity is detected on the sides of the tongue.

balanced A wine with all its components (mainly acidity, alcohol, fruit, tannins, sugar, and extract) in harmony, with no one element prominent.

big A full-bodied wine that leaves a major impression on the senses, typically containing high levels of fruit, tannins, and/or alcohol. Also used to mean plenty of flavor.

bitter Normally a negative term used to describe a wine with an excess of harsh tannins, which leaves a bitter taste in the mouth, detected at the back of the tongue. In some reds, however, a certain amount of bitterness is a desirable characteristic.

blockbuster Used to describe exceptionally "big" wines. Think large amounts of fruit, alcohol, tannins, or oaky flavors.

body The weight or feel of wine in the mouth, determined by its alcohol and extract. To work out whether a wine is light-, medium-, or full-bodied, it may be useful to compare it to the feel of water.

clean Lacking faults in terms of aroma and flavor.

complex A wine with many layers of aroma and flavor—many different fruits, plus characteristics such as spice and vanilla. Complexity is one of the elements that separates an average wine from a good or great one. The most complex wines have typically gone through a period of ageing, allowing more flavors to develop.

concentrated An intense taste, normally found in wines with high levels of tannin, sugar, and flavoring and coloring compounds.

crisp Noticeable acidity but in a positive, refreshing way. Usually used for white wines with clean, fresh flavors.

dry No obvious sugar or sweetness in the wine. Note that very ripe, fruity flavors and new oak flavors can sometimes give the impression of sweetness, although the wine itself can still be dry. "Dried-out" is a term given to red wines that have spent too long in barrel or bottle and have lost their fruit flavor.

easy-drinking A relatively simple wine that can be enjoyed without much thought. It will be fruity and, if red, low in tannin.

elegant A subjective term, used to describe a good quality, subtle, balanced wine which is not too fruity, and is extremely pleasant to drink.

extract All the solid matter in a wine such as tannins, sugars, and coloring and flavoring compounds. Extract is what gives a wine its body.

finesse Quality of a wine that displays elegance.

flabby A negative term used for a wine that has low acidity and is therefore unbalanced. It can make for a slightly cloying taste.

fleshy A wine that feels almost solid in texture when in the mouth, thanks to high levels of fruit and extract.

fresh Like crisp, noticeably acidic in an attractive, refreshing way. Normally used for young white wines.

fruity A wine with plenty of attractive fruit flavors.

harsh Rough around the edges, lacking in subtlety.

heavy Normally refers to a full-bodied, tannic red wine, and means it is tough to drink or heavy going. It may indicate that the wine needs to spend further time in bottle.

mature Ready to drink. Generally used for quality wines that require time in bottle. Over-mature is a euphemism for past its best.

oaky Normally a negative term to describe when oak flavors dominate other flavors in a wine. If the wine is young and good quality, it may lose some of its oakiness with a few years in bottle. Oak flavors can be desirable, but only if they are balanced by fruit.

powerful A "big" wine with high levels of extract and/or alcohol. Can be used in a positive or negative sense.

racy Word similar in meaning to crisp and fresh, used to describe wines with noticeable levels of refreshing acidity. It is especially associated with Riesling.

For more details on New Zealand grape varieties **See p108**

rich Like concentrated, implying deep, intense flavors in the mouth. Can also be used to mean slightly sweet.

ripe Wine made from ripe grapes and showing flavors of richer, warmer-climate fruits, such as pineapples (rather than apples). Ripe wine might also suggest a certain sweetness, even though it may not contain sugar.

simple Lacking complexity, with one-dimensional flavors. This is a fault in expensive wine, but it may not be a problem for everyday drinking wine.

soft A red wine with gentle tannins. Also known as smooth.

structured Normally refers to the tannins in a red wine, which support the other elements. In a "well-structured" wine the tannins are noticeable but still balanced. Sometimes used for acidity in white wines, for example a wine can be described as having a "good acidic structure."

subtle Normally linked to finesse, it means a wine contains a number of different nuances and tastes. It can also be a euphemism for a wine lacking in fruity flavors.

sweet A wine with noticeable levels of sugar, detected by the tip of the tongue. The phrase "sweet fruit flavors" may be used to describe an extremely ripe style of wine.

tannic An excess of tannins, the drying compounds that come from the skins, seeds, and stalks of grapes. Some tannic wines simply require further maturation in bottle. Tannins are not necessarily a bad thing, they just tend to be balanced by fruity flavors.

up-front Used to describe an easy-drinking style of wine with straightforward, fruity flavors.

warm A wine with an excess of alcohol leaves a "warm" finish. Can be used to describe full-bodied, spicy red wines.

Aromas and Flavors

There are obviously thousands of different identifiable aromas and flavors in wine, but here is a list of some of those most commonly detected. Certain flavors (such as blackcurrant) speak for themselves, whereas others, such as "mineral" or "vegetal," require a little explanation. Entries include examples of grape varieties or wines where the flavor is usually encountered.

apple Often found in cooler-climate, dry white wines, such as those from the South Island of New Zealand.

apricot Common in riper styles of white wine such as Viognier and oak-fermented Chardonnay.

blackcurrant Widely associated with Cabernet Sauvignon and some other red grape varieties such as Merlot, Syrah/Shiraz, and Cabernet Franc. Occasionally a certain underripe blackcurrant flavor can be detected in Sauvignon Blanc.

buttery A creamy texture reminiscent of butter (rather than a specific flavor) is commonly found in oak-fermented Chardonnay and other white wines. This is caused by malolactic fermentation in the barrel, particularly where lees stirring is used.

cherry Widely found in red wines, especially in cool-climate Pinot Noir.

citrus A character widely found in white wines, particularly fresh, aromatic styles. Can be further narrowed down to lemon, lime, orange etc.

coconut A flavor commonly associated with both whites and reds that have been fermented or matured in new American oak barrels. In excess, it can indicate a fault.

creamy Used to indicate a smooth, quite full-bodied texture in a wine, or a smell of cream.

diesel Widely found in mature bottles of Riesling, particularly in older German examples. It tends to occur earlier in Australian Riesling.

earthy A soil-like aroma commonly identified in older bottles of red Bordeaux.

farmyard A slightly dirty, earthy, manure-type aroma. In a young wine, it may indicate poor (unclean) winemaking practices. In an older bottle of red Burgundy, it can be a desirable, developed character.

floral A number of cool-climate whites display aromas vaguely reminiscent of flowers. Some are easy to identify, such as elderflower (aromatic whites), violets (mature Bordeaux), and roses (Gewürztraminer).

game/gaminess A decaying, fleshy aroma commonly associated with older bottles of Pinot Noir, Syrah/Shiraz, and other mature red wines.

gooseberry A classic flavor of Sauvignon Blanc. Also found in other aromatic, zesty white wines.

grapey A term meaning smelling of grapes, a vaguely "sweet" fruity aroma. The only variety for which this is true is Muscat (and all its various names and clones).

grass Widely found in fresh, aromatic wines from cooler climates from grapes such as Sauvignon Blanc, Semillon, and Chenin Blanc.

honey Normally found in sweeter styles of wine, particularly when the grapes have been affected by botrytis.

jammy A slightly derogatory term for a red wine bursting with up-front flavors of blackcurrant, raspberry, and other fruits, but lacking in structure. It normally implies the wine lacks finesse.

lemon Widely found in white wines, particularly those from cooler climates.

liquorice Commonly associated with full-bodied reds made from Syrah/Shiraz grapes.

lychee An aroma widely found in wines made from Gewürztraminer.

mineral It is difficult to taste mineral but the term is usually used to describe a sharp, earthy character in cool-climate wines such as Sauvignon Blanc from New Zealand's South Island.

mint Particularly associated with Cabernet Sauvignon grown in warm-climate countries.

mushroom An aroma displayed by Pinot Noir as it matures.

pepper (black) Commonly associated with powerful red wines, especially those made of the Syrah/Shiraz and Grenache grape varieties.

plum Apparent in many red wines, but particularly those made from Merlot.

rose Found in Gewürztraminer and wines made from the Nebbiolo grape variety.

rubber Can indicate a wine fault caused by excessive sulfur, or is widely (and positively) associated with Australian reds made of the Syrah/Shiraz grape variety.

spice Found in wines fermented and matured in new oak barrels. Also apparent in certain red grape varieties, such as Grenache (which often has a peppery flavor).

summer fruits Aromas such as strawberry, raspberry, and cherry. Especially associated with young Pinot Noir.

tangy Similar to zesty, but perhaps with more orange fruits. Mostly applies to whites.

tobacco A mature, developed aroma found in older bottles of Cabernet Sauvignon, particularly red Bordeaux.

toast The word "toasty" is most frequently used to describe the aroma imparted by oak barrels, but "toastiness" is also a quality of mature Champagne, especially *blanc de blancs*. It may also be displayed by Sémillons from Australia's Hunter Valley.

tropical fruits Ripe flavors such as banana, pineapple, and mango that are normally used to describe Australian Chardonnay.

vanilla Derived directly from new oak barrels. The wood contains vanillin, the chemical compound that gives vanilla pods their distinctive aroma.

vegetal Rotting vegetable-type aromas found in older bottles of red and white wines, especially Burgundy (of both colors). It might sound unpleasant, but it is a desirable attribute in these styles of wine.

yeast Bread-type aroma widely associated with Champagne (and the secondary fermentation process used to create it).

zesty Aromas of lemon, lime and, sometimes, orange. Normally found in crisp, refreshing dry white wines, especially those from New Zealand.

Common Faults

Wine today is much more reliable than ever before. With the exception of a corked bottle, seriously flawed wine is relatively rare. There are, however, a number of problems you may be unlucky enough to encounter, which would warrant your returning a bottle of wine to the place of purchase.

corked This is the most common wine fault, found in 2 to 5 percent of all wines sold. It is caused by a mold found in some natural corks that can taint the wine, and has nothing to do with pieces of cork floating in your glass. Corked wine smells musty and lacks fruit flavors, but this may not become obvious until it has spent a few minutes in the glass. Plastic corks or screwcaps eliminate this problem.

oxidized Over-exposure to oxygen harms wine, eventually turning it into vinegar. A wine may become oxidized if its seal is insufficiently airtight, if left too long in bottle before opening, or if left too long once opened.

sulfur All wines are bottled with a dose of sulfur, which acts as a preservative. However, if too much sulfur is added, the wine acquires an astringent, rubbery smell. In large quantities, it can be dangerous for asthmatics.

poor winemaking If you taste a wine with excess acidity, tannins, or oak, or with an absence of fruity flavors, it may simply be the result of poor winemaking.

Wine and Food Matching

Wine and food have complemented each other for thousands of years. Wine comes into its own at the dinner table thanks to its moderate alcohol, refreshing acidity, and sheer range of flavors. It is worth knowing some successful pairings of food and wine that have stood the test of time.

Guidelines

Whether selecting a bottle to accompany a take-out, or choosing different wines for each course at a dinner party, there are a number of basic guidelines

• Decide on the dominant taste and choose a wine to accompany it.

• Select a wine to match the weight and power of your food. Full-flavored foods require full-flavored, full-bodied wines. Delicate dishes are overpowered by heavily oaked or tannic styles, so they require light wines. Full-bodied whites have similar power and weight to lighter reds, so work equally well with dishes such as grilled tuna or roast turkey.

• Sweet food should be matched by a similarly sweet wine. Many Thai dishes, for example, contain a lot of sugar, which is why off-dry styles such as Gewürztraminer work so well.

• Tannins in a red wine taste softer when drunk with red meat. This is why classic combinations like beef with red Bordeaux are so effective.

• The more complicated the flavors in a dish, the more difficult it is to find a wine to pair with it, though some wines do work well with a range of flavors *(See In Restaurants p144)*.

• If serving top-quality wine, simply prepared dishes using the finest ingredients allow the wine to take center stage.

• Try to match regional dishes with the same region's wines.

Apéritifs

An apéritif should simply whet your appetite, leaving you ready to enjoy the food and wine to come, so never choose anything too heavy or overbearing.

• Dry, light, and refreshing white wine works well. Avoid oaked wine. Think unoaked Semillon or a dry Riesling.

• Champagne and traditional-method sparkling wines are ideal, particularly for special occasions. Their dryness and relative acidity stimulates the tastebuds.

• Do not serve the best wine of the evening as an apéritif. A well-made, basic bottle will allow true appreciation of the subtleties of the better wines to follow.

With Appetizers

Bear in mind the best order for serving wine when choosing your appetizer— white before red, dry before sweet, lighter-before fuller-bodied, and in ascending order of quality. If the choice of menu requires a full-bodied red for the appetizer, avoid a dish that needs a light white for the entree.

Asparagus Sauvignon Blanc. If served in a creamy sauce, a fuller-bodied wine such as Semillon.

Foie gras A Sauternes-style botrytized wine, although serving a sweet wine this early in the meal could present problems later. Champagne and Gewürztraminer also work.

Gazpacho Relatively neutral, dry whites.

Pâtés and terrines A wine that works with the main ingredient in its cooked form *(See Fish and Meat sections)*.

Salad (no dressing) Sauvignon Blanc, Riesling, and unoaked Chardonnay are good options.

Salad (with creamy dressing) Chardonnay or Pinot Blanc.

Salad (with vinaigrette) A wine with high acidity like Sauvignon Blanc, or dry Riesling.

Soup (chicken) Medium-bodied Chardonnay or Pinot Blanc.

Soup (chunky, meaty) Inexpensive reds (Merlot or Cabernet-Merlot blends).

Soup (creamy and fishy) Fuller-flavored Chardonnay or a Semillon-Sauvignon Blanc from Western Australia. Sparkling wines can also work well, as can light rosés.

With Fish & Seafood

The dominant flavor in seafood dishes will often be the sauce. Creamy dishes demand a full-bodied white, whereas tomato-based ones require a medium-bodied red. Also consider the intensity of the cooking method, and the quality of the ingredients.

Bouillabaisse Inexpensive whites, reds, and rosés.

Chowder (creamy) Basic Chardonnay.

Chowder (tomato-based) Medium-bodied reds.

Cod (battered) Crisp, dry whites, such as Sauvignon Blanc or Chenin Blanc.

Cod and haddock (fresh) Unoaked Chardonnay.

Crab Sauvignon Blanc or a dry Riesling.
Lobster Good-quality Chardonnay.
Mackerel and sardines (fresh) Sauvignon Blanc, or light rosés.
Mackerel (smoked) Pinot Gris or medium Riesling.
Mussels/Oysters A good Sauvignon Blanc from Marlborough or the Adelaide Hills.
Salmon (barbecued) Lighter reds such as a New Zealand Pinot Noir.
Salmon (grilled) Unoaked Chardonnay, Semillon, or Pinot Blanc. Dry Riesling is also a decent match.
Salmon (poached) A delicate Chardonnay or good Semillon-Sauvignon.
Salmon (smoked) Sauvignon Blanc or dry Riesling. Champagne-style sparkling wines also work well.
Sea bass (with butter sauce) A good-quality Chardonnay.
Sea bass (with tomato sauce) Light- or medium-bodied reds.
Trout (fresh) Pinot Blanc or unoaked Chardonnay.
Trout (smoked) A good Chardonnay.
Tuna (fresh) Fuller-bodied, dry white such as Semillon or light to medium red such as a New Zealand Pinot Noir.
Turbot Good quality Chardonnay, or Hunter Valley Semillon.

With White Meats

In general, white meat has a relatively neutral flavor. Take note of the recipe used when selecting a wine to show it off.
Chicken (barbecued) Chardonnay, Sauvignon Blanc, or light red wines.
Chicken (creamy sauce) Semillon, Riesling, or oaked Chenin Blanc.
Chicken (roast) Chardonnay, Pinot Noir, or soft Merlot.

Coq au vin Good-quality Pinot Noir from New Zealand or Victoria.
Pork (roast) A range of wines from Chardonnay and Sauvignon Blanc through to lighter reds like basic Merlot or Pinot Noir.
Pork (spare ribs) A fruity South Australian Shiraz or Shiraz-based blend.
Pork sausages Inexpensive reds.
Turkey (plain roast) Oaked Chardonnay or a light red wine like soft Merlot and Pinot Noir.
Turkey (with cranberry sauce/stuffing) Good Margaret River Cabernet Sauvignon or Cabernet-Merlot blend.
Veal Dry whites such as unoaked Chardonnay or a soft fruity red like Merlot.

With Red Meats, Barbecues, & Game

These meats call for fuller-bodied styles of wine. Beef and lamb in particular tend to be complemented by tannic red wines. However, the sauces served also affect the choice.
Barbecues Powerful reds such as Shiraz or Cabernet-Shiraz blends.
Beef (hamburgers, steak au poivre, or in pastry) Powerful Shiraz from South Australia or New South Wales.
Beef (roast beef or steak) Full-bodied Shiraz, Cabernet, or Cabernet-Shiraz blend.
Beef (with wine sauce) A good-quality New Zealand Pinot Noir.
Duck (roast) A good-quality Pinot Noir from Victoria or New Zealand's South Island.
Duck (with apple/orange sauce) Aromatic Riesling.
Game A good-quality Cabernet Sauvignon .
Lamb (casseroles and stews) Spicy reds such as a peppery Shiraz or Shiraz-based blend.

Lamb (chops) Good Cabernet Sauvignon or Cabernet-Merlot blend.
Lamb (roast) Top-quality Coonawarra Cabernet Sauvignon.

With Vegetarian Dishes

Vegetarians and vegans may find some wines unsuitable due to animal products used in them. Consult the back label or ask the retailer to pinpoint vegetarian- or vegan-friendly wine. It can be difficult to pair vegetarian food with top Chardonnay or full-bodied reds, but mushroom and pumpkin risotto stand up to the challenge.
Lentil- and vegetable-based casseroles Basic South Australian reds.
Mushroom risotto Good Cabernet Sauvignon.
Pasta (creamy sauce) Unoaked Chardonnay, Pinot Blanc, or Semillon.
Pasta (tomato-based sauce) Light red such as Pinot Noir.
Pumpkin or butternut squash risotto Good-quality Chardonnay.
Quiches and omelettes Unoaked Chardonnay, Pinot Blanc, or light red like Pinot Noir.
Soy-based nuggets and tofu Choose a wine according to the flavor of the ingredients they are cooked with, as they tend to take on the same flavor.
Vegetarian chilli Hearty reds such as a fruity Merlot.
Vegetarian lasagne (with tofu) Full-bodied whites such as Chardonnay or Pinot Gris.
Vegetable tarts, pies, and pasties Spicy reds such as a peppery Shiraz.
Veggie burgers Full-bodied Shiraz or Cabernet-Shiraz blend as these dishes can taste quite "meaty."

 Vegetarians and vegans should note that gelatin, isinglass (made from fish), and egg whites are sometimes used to fine (clarify) wines

Reference–Wine and Food Matching

With Ethnic Dishes

Chinese Riesling, Gewürztraminer, Pinot Gris, or Sauvignon Blanc.

Indian With mild dishes, an inexpensive Chardonnay. With medium-hot dishes, a soft, fruity red such as Merlot or Malbec. With really hot and spicy dishes, avoid wine and choose beer, water, or lassi instead.

Japanese (sushi) A "rice wine" such as saké is traditional.

Japanese (teriyaki sauces) Fruity reds such as Merlot or Malbec.

Thai (curry) Inexpensive Sauvignon Blanc.

Thai (general) Off-dry white such as Riesling or Gewürztraminer.

With Desserts

Always try to select a wine that is sweeter than your dessert. You can also choose a wine with a slightly higher alcohol content here as it is the end of the meal. Intensely flavored desserts are well complemented by powerful, fortified styles.

Chocolate cake Select your wine depending on the richness of the chocolate. The orange flavors in certain Australian Muscats can work sensationally.

Crème brûlée Botrytized dessert wine makes a classic partnership.

Fruit A wide variety, such as sweeter styles of Riesling, Semillon, or Chenin Blanc.

Fruit tarts and pies Choose a wine based on the dominant flavor—normally the fruit itself.

Ice cream Thick, sticky styles like Liqueur Muscat.

With Cheeses

Cheese and wine can be a wonderful combination, but pairing them is not as easy as many people think. The diverse flavors and textures of different cheeses mean that anything from a sweet white to a fortified red can be served successfully.

Blue cheeses A sweet wine is generally required. Roquefort and Sauternes-style dessert wine is a classic combination.

Brie Light, fruity reds.

Camembert Light and fruity reds, but can also be paired with whites such as Chardonnay.

Goat's cheese Sauvignon Blanc from Marlborough or Martinborough.

Gruyère and Emmenthal Red wines such as Shiraz, Cabernet-Shiraz blends, or Merlot. However, Riesling can work well, too.

Mature Cheddar Good Margaret River Cabernet Sauvignon or tawny port.

Mozzarella Unoaked Chardonnay.

Sheep's cheese Sweeter styles of white wine like Riesling and Muscat, as well as spicy reds.

Traditional English hard cheeses Cool-climate, dry whites such as Sauvignon Blanc or Chenin Blanc.

Social Occasions

With food The general rules of wine and food matching still apply. It is often wise to select generally food-friendly wines (see In Restaurants below), as guests are then able to enjoy one wine with all the canapés and different courses served.

Without food In general, wines to be enjoyed on their own should be light and unpretentious. For parties and social events where no food is on offer, steer clear of anything too full-bodied and avoid high acidity or powerful tannins. Also take the time of year and weather into account.

In summer Choose crisp, refreshing wines like Riesling, Chenin Blanc, and other cool-climate, relatively low-alcohol whites. You could also go for light, fruity reds suitable for a brief chilling. Basic Merlot, and Pinot Noir are good choices.

In winter A medium-bodied wine, whether red or white, focusing on bright, fruity flavors and avoiding lots of oak. Good bets are Semillon, unoaked Chardonnay, and Pinot Blanc. Reds such as Cabernet-Shiraz or Cabernet-Merlot blends are also highly enjoyable at this time of year.

At celebrations Champagne and sparkling wines are the classic choices. Champagne tends to be more expensive, so is generally only an option for those with a bigger budget. Other sparkling wines can work very well, however, and are normally a better choice to use in cocktails such as mimosas.

In Restaurants

Many top restaurants have a sommelier to offer diners advice on wine. If no sommelier is on hand, there are a few types of wine that are good with most foods. If you are all ordering different dishes, half bottles can help everyone get something to complement their particular meal.

• Opt for medium-bodied styles, avoiding extremes. For whites, unoaked Chardonnay, Semillon, Pinot Gris, or Sauvignon Blanc are the most versatile. Among the reds, Pinot Noir, inexpensive Merlot, or a fruity Cabernet-Merlot blend are excellent choices.

• If the restaurant focuses on a particular nationality or style of cooking, try to choose wines of the same nationality.

Buying Wine

There has never been so much choice when it comes to buying wine in the United States. However, due to controls implemented following the repeal of Prohibition, each state has its own laws as to how, when, and where alcohol can be sold. Therefore, selection, availability, and price vary widely.

Supermarkets

Supermarkets are a reliable, if not especially adventurous, source of wine. In states where the sale of wine in supermarkets and grocery stores is legal, most major food chains have a selection designed to appeal to a broad range of tastes. While large supermarkets tend not to stock obscure styles or wine from boutique producers, some smaller specialty grocery stores offer a wider, more interesting selection.

Discount Stores

In states where they are allowed to sell wine, stores such as Sam's Club, Costco, and Target have a wide selection of basic brands at very reasonable prices. Although these types of stores lack a sales force able to answer wine-related questions, they offer excellent value. Costco and Sam's Club provide a good selection of high-end wines at very attractive prices, but bargain hunters should be aware that availability varies dramatically from week to week and popular wines are soon sold out .

Wine Merchants

The legal structure of selling wine in the United States means that there is no national chain that can sell wine in every state. As a result, there are hundreds of specialty wine merchants, each with a different selection and focus. This makes them the destination of choice for discerning wine lovers. They have much to offer in terms of advice and ranges of wines from small, high-quality producers. Owners and staff often have tasted most of the wines and are happy to share their knowledge. Take time to discuss your requirements and preferences: price, styles of wines you enjoy, and the food with which you plan to drink the wine.

Direct from the Winery

With wineries in 50 states, people can buy wine made in their own backyard. Although there may be little difference in price between the winery and a store, buying wine directly from a producer often means you can get hold of older vintages or wines not sold in stores. Depending on state laws, it is possible to order wine directly from a winery and have it shipped to your home. To find out more about wine shipping laws visit the site of the Wine and Spirit Wholesalers of America *(www.wswa.org)*.

Auctions

It is not without risk, but buying at an auction or internet exchange can be an excellent way of acquiring cases of wine, particularly older, rarer vintages. Major auction houses such as Christie's *(www.christies.com)* and Sotheby's *(www.sothebys. com)* hold regular wine sales, as do smaller, local houses. Be aware of commission fees (10 to 15 percent on top of the price of the lot) and learn as much as possible about the condition and provenance of lots before bidding on them.

Wine on the Web

Many wine merchants and wineries sell on the internet, and there are also some virtual-only stores. Wine.com, the largest on-line retailer, offers a wide variety of wines, some that are difficult to find elsewhere. Shipping cost can be high and some states do not permit wine to be shipped directly to consumers.

Selected Retailers

BOSTON
Federal Wine & Spirits
(617) 367 8605
Marty's Liquors
(617) 782 3250

CHICAGO
Sam's Wine & Spirits
(312) 664 4394
Wine Discount Center
(312) 489 3454

LOS ANGELES
Wally's Wine & Spirits
(310) 475 0606
Woodland Hills Wine
(800) 678 9643

NEW YORK
Astor Wine & Spirits
(212) 674 7500
Zachys
(800) 723 0241

SEATTLE
McCarthy & Schiering
(206) 524 9500
Pike & Western Wine
(206) 441 1307

WASHINGTON, D.C.
MacArthur Beverages
(202) 338 1433

Storing and Serving Wine

Over the years, wine has become associated with a number of procedures, like cellaring, breathing, and decanting. While it is not strictly essential to know anything about these terms to enjoy wine, an understanding of these practices can maximize the pleasure gained from both buying and drinking it.

Storing Wine

Most wines sold today are made to be enjoyed young. Almost all mid-priced bottles will survive in a rack for around 12 months, but are likely to deteriorate if left for longer. Traditionally, most wines worth cellaring were from the Old World, but age-worthy bottles are now created by the finest producers elsewhere, too. If in any doubt, it is always better to drink a wine too young rather than too old.

Wine is best stored on its side—constant contact between cork and liquid prevents the cork from drying out. Sparkling wines and wines with a screwcap can be stored upright because this problem does not arise. If you want to cellar wine but lack the ideal conditions, there are alternatives: buying a wine fridge or cabinet that holds bottles in perfect storage conditions; or paying for dedicated storage with a professional firm. Contact your local wine merchant for advice.

Cellars

A cellar can range from a humble, under-stair cupboard to a vast underground labyrinth, as long as conditions are right for maturation. Key considerations when choosing the perfect "cellar" are as follows:
• A constant temperature between 50 and 59°F (10 and 15°C) is preferable. A bit higher than this is not a major concern: the wine will mature more quickly, but slightly less favorably. It is temperature variation that causes most harm.
• Wine dislikes light, which is why many bottles are made of colored glass. Dark rooms or sealed boxes are best.
• A lack of moisture can cause corks to dry out, contract, and let air into the bottle, oxidizing the wine and eventually turning it into vinegar. Slightly damp cellars, on the other hand, will not harm the wine.
• Excess movement or vibration can damage wine, so avoid storage next to fridges and washing machines, and also avoid handling or unnecessary transport.

Effects of Ageing

As wines sit in the bottle, a series of chemical reactions changes relatively simple fruity flavors to more developed, complex tastes. In reds, the color becomes lighter, the tannins get softer, and the wine takes on aromas such as cedar, leather, or mushrooms. Whites, on the other hand, deepen in color, and become less sweet and more intense. Typical aromas of a mature white wine include nuts, wax, and even diesel. The effects of oak barrels—hints of vanilla, coconut, and spice—lessen in all wines as they mature.

Serving Temperature

The correct temperature is extremely important to the taste of wine. White wines are often served too cold, and reds too warm. Some guidelines to follow:
• Sparkling wines: Cool temperatures of around 46°F (8°C).
• Light, aromatic whites: Quite cold—around 50°F (10°C) or a few hours in the fridge. Chilling emphasizes the crisp, fresh taste and does not dull the aromas.
• White Burgundy and other Chardonnays: These are less aromatic, so serve around 54°F (12°C).
• Light- and medium-bodied reds: Chill slightly to around 54 or 55°F (12 or 13°C) (half an hour in the fridge), particularly in summer.
• Full-bodied reds: Low temperatures emphasize the tannins in the wine, so serve these reasonably warm, around 59°F (15°C).

Serving Order

There are a number of generally accepted rules for serving wine:
• White before red—although a light-bodied red can be enjoyed before a full-bodied white.
• Dry before sweet whites—this avoids making the wine taste excessively acidic.
• Light reds before heavy reds—lighter wines tend to taste thin after a heavier example.
• Lower quality wines before special ones. There is no clear consensus on whether young or old wines should be consumed first. Much depends on the individual wines in question.

Reference—Storing and Serving Wine

Decanting

Certain high-quality wines (mostly reds), such as a 2000 Bordeaux, opened before their peak, can benefit greatly from exposure to oxygen in the air—or breathing—before drinking. Simply pulling the cork on a bottle and allowing it to stand open is unlikely to make much difference. Using a decanter, however, will. The shape of the vessel used makes very little difference, as long as it is made of glass and open-topped.

Another reason to use a decanter is to separate a wine from its sediment or deposit, especially if it is unfiltered. Wines that "throw" a sediment include vintage port, unfiltered or traditional LBV port, crusted port, and older vintages of full-bodied reds.

To decant a wine, stand the bottle upright for at least 24 hours to allow the sediment to fall to the bottom. Then, pull the cork and, with a source of light, either a lighted candle or a naked light bulb, behind the neck to allow you to see the contents, slowly pour the wine into the decanter. Stop when you see the sediment reach the neck of the bottle. Do not leave wine in a decanter for long, as prolonged exposure to oxygen will ruin it.

Opening Fizz

The correct procedure for opening a sparkling wine or Champagne is as follows:
• Hold the bottle at an angle of approximately 55 degrees to the horizontal.
• Point the neck of the bottle away from other people and from breakables.
• Carefully remove the foil and wire muzzle.
• Holding the bottle in one hand and the cork in the other, twist the bottle (not the cork) until it eases with a satisfying pop.

Glasses

Using the correct wine glasses can influence the taste of a wine. Although you can buy individual glass designs for different wines, a good all-purpose wine glass will normally suffice. This should have a stem so that you do not have to handle the bowl; and the bowl should be large enough to hold a decent measure, yet still allow room for the wine to be swirled. The bowl should be narrower at the rim than at the base, directing the aromas toward your nose. Finally, clear glass—not cut, colored, or patterned—allows the color of the wine to show through. The only major styles that require a different shape of glass are Champagne and sparkling wines. Their tall, straight, thin glasses are specifically designed to show off and retain the bubbles.

How Much per Person?

Serving quantities depend on the occasion and, of course, the drinking capacities of your guests. At dinner parties, estimate between half a bottle and a whole bottle of wine per person per evening. When ordering large amounts of wine for an event, remember that many retailers operate a sale or return policy, which allows you to return unopened bottles. In this instance, always err on the generous side when ordering.

Leftover Wine

Leftover wine should be poured into the smallest appropriate bottle size, sealed with the original cork if possible, and kept in the fridge. It should be finished off within 24 to 48 hours, as deterioration will quickly set in.

Red and White Wines to Keep

Keeping times depend on the quality of the producer, vineyard site, and vintage. Bear in mind that only the finest wines can age for longer periods:

Whites
Chardonnay: 2 to 5 years for top Australian examples.
Riesling: 2 years for low-priced wines; up to 5 for the best Australian ones; sweeter styles keep longer than drier.
Sauvignon Blanc: 2 to 3 years for best wines from Marlborough, New Zealand.
Semillon: 1 to 2 years for low-priced wines; 5 to 20 years for the best Hunter Valley examples.
Sweet wine: up to 10 years for the best wines from Australia and New Zealand.

Reds
Cabernet Sauvignon-based wines: 3 to 10 years for the best Australian wines (5 to 20 years for Bordeaux).
Merlot: 2 to 8 years for the best Australian and New Zealand wines (3 to 15 years for good Bordeaux).
Pinot Noir: 2 to 8 years for the best examples from Central Otago and Martinborough, New Zealand.
Syrah: 5 to 15 years for the best wines.

Reference—Storing and Serving Wine

Glossary

Like any other specialist subject, wine has its own unique vocabulary. This glossary includes common terms originating in France and other Old World countries, as well terms that are specific to winemaking in Australia and New Zealand.

A

acid/acidity All wines contain various acids, including tartaric, malic, and citric. Acidity is an essential element in wine, helping to maintain freshness and balance—too much, and it can taste unduly sharp, too little, and a "flabby," cloying wine will result.

acidification The addition of chemical acids to the must during winemaking to compensate for a lack of natural acidity in the grapes.

ageing Most wines are designed to be enjoyed as soon as they are released. However, a proportion will improve in bottle if stored in a cool, dark place. Full-bodied reds, sweet whites, and fortified wines can all benefit from ageing.

American oak Wood originating from forests of the eastern US, used to make oak barrels. Popular in North and South America, Spain, and Australia, American oak barrels tend to impart a more powerful vanilla flavor than their European counterparts.

appellation A legally defined area where grapes are grown and wine is produced, sometimes used as a shortened version of AOC or AC.

Appellation d'Origine Contrôlée or **AOC** (French) Also known as Appellation Contrôlée (AC). The highest quality classification for wines produced in France. It guarantees that a bottle has been made in a specific region, according to local regulations. Not all AOC or

AC wines are good quality, but on average, they should be better (though not necessarily better value) than wines with a lower classification such as *vin de pays* or *vin de table*.

B

barrel Barrels or casks can be used at several stages of winemaking. Better quality whites may be fermented in barrel to produce subtle and complex wood flavors. Maturation in barrel helps to soften the wine and, if the oak is new, pick up aromas of cedar or vanilla. "Barrel select" may imply quality, but has no legal definition. *See also* **American oak** and **French oak**.

barrel-aged Term describing a wine that has been matured in oak barrels, a process that softens its taste and possibly adds oak flavors.

barrel-fermented This indicates a wine has been fermented in an oak barrel. Normally applicable to white wines, the process helps to integrate oak flavors.

barrique (French) Originally a small oak cask or barrel holding 60 gallons (225 liters) of wine. Now often used to describe any small oak cask.

base wine The still wine used to create champagne and other sparkling wine.

bin Originally a collection or stack of wine bottles. It is commonly found on wine labels, to signify different brands of wine.

biodynamism An extreme form of organic viticulture

that emphasizes the health of the soil. Some of its methods may sound bizarre, but a number of world-class wines are produced using this approach.

blanc de blancs (French) White wine made entirely from white grapes. The term is commonly used for Champagne and other sparkling wines.

blanc de noirs (French) White wine made entirely from red grapes, usually applied to Champagne and other sparkling wines.

blend A mixture of wines of different grape varieties, styles, origin, or age, contrived to improve the balance of the wine or maintain a constant style.

Bordeaux A wine from the Bordeaux region of France made using the grape varieties and/or techniques common in this area. Bordeaux is a famously full-bodied red wine made from a blend of Cabernet Sauvignon, Merlot, Cabernet Franc, Malbec, and Petit Verdot which is often matured in oak barrels. It can age for decades.

botrytis A vine disease, also known as noble rot, responsible for some of the world's greatest dessert wines. In the correct conditions, the fungus (*Botrytis cinerea*) produces shriveled, sugar-rich grapes that can be fermented into a naturally sweet and intensely flavored wine.

bottle fermentation The technique that gives champagne its "fizz." After a normal fermentation, still wine is placed into a bottle with sugar and yeast. A secondary fermentation begins, producing carbon dioxide gas inside the bottle and creating a sparkling wine. The term is normally used by sparkling wine producers outside the Champagne region.

Bourgogne The French

Reference–Glossary

word for Burgundy.

brut (French) Means dry. Normally used to describe Champagne and other sparkling white wines.

Burgundy A wine from the Burgundy region of France, made using the grape varieties and/or the techniques common in this region. Burgundy is world famous for its dry whites made from Chardonnay and medium-bodied reds made from Pinot Noir.

C

canopy All parts of the vine that are visible above the ground, including the trunk, leaves, shoots, stems, and grapes.

canopy management The practice of manipulating the vine and its canopy to ensure that the grapes and leaves are correctly exposed to the sun. It also aims to ensure a good circulation of air through the vine, helping to prevent fungal diseases. Canopy management includes training and pruning.

carbonic maceration Winemaking technique associated with Beaujolais in France. The grapes are fermented as whole berries, producing a deep colored, fruity wine, light in tannin.

Certified Origin or **CO** The appellation system in operation in New Zealand since 1996.

chaptalization The practice of increasing alcohol levels through the addition of sugar during winemaking. Common in cooler wine regions where the climate may struggle to produce sufficient natural sugar in the grapes.

château (French) Used to denote a French winegrowing/producing estate. The term is widely used in Bordeaux.

claret A uniquely English term for red Bordeaux.

clone A group of vines all descended from a single parent vine using cuttings or buds. They are genetically identical to the parent plant and are usually selected for characteristics such as fine flavor or good color.

CO see **Certified Origin**.

cold fermentation Slow fermentation at low temperatures to extract freshness and fruit flavor from the grapes.

cooperative Organization collectively owned by its members. Typically wine cooperatives consist of a number of growers who join together for winemaking and marketing purposes. Quality can vary from good to extremely poor.

corked Wine that has been affected by a moldy, musty taint from a defective natural cork. The wine may be stripped of its normal fruit flavors and can have a slightly bitter taste. It is believed that around six percent of wines using natural corks are corked, and many producers and retailers have consequently changed over to screwcaps

and synthetic stoppers.

côte(s)/coteaux (French) Hill or hillside.

crémant (French) Indicates a sparkling wine produced outside the Champagne region, but using the same methods as Champagne.

cru (French) Literally "growth" or "vineyard." Hence *cru classé* means classified vineyard. *Cru bourgeois* is a classification for estates in Bordeaux's Médoc appellation. *See also* **premier cru** and **grand cru**.

cuvée (French) Normally used to mean blend. Wine labels that say *cuvée de prestige* or *tête de cuvée* are no guarantee of quality. In Champagne, *cuvée* denotes the first and finest juice to come from the press.

cuvée de prestige (French) Term, normally associated with Champagne, referring to a top quality, luxury wine from the best vineyards and matured for many years before release. Examples include Dom Pérignon from Moët & Chandon and La Grande Dame from Veuve Clicquot Ponsardin.

Key Climatic Terms

continental climate A climate characterized by extreme temperature variations across the year. Usually found in regions well away from the influence of water (sea or lakes). Cold winters and hot summers are the norm.

degree days A unit devised to measure the suitability of climates for viticulture.

macroclimate The overall climate within a region.

maritime climate A climate that is influenced by a large body of water, typically a sea or lake. Temperatures will tend to remain relatively stable across the year with mild winters and warm summers.

marginal climate A climate that is barely sufficient to permit viticulture. Normally applied to weather that is too cold rather than too warm. Expect regions with a marginal climate to have wide variations in quality between vintages.

mesoclimate The climate in a small district or even an individual vineyard.

microclimate A specific climate within a very small area.

moderate climate A climate with only minimal temperature variation over the course of the year. Most commonly found near a large body of water. *See* maritime climate.

D

decanting The process of pouring wine from its original bottle into another vessel or decanter. The technique is normally used for old or unfiltered wines to separate the liquid from the sediment deposited in the bottle. It can also be used for younger wines, to allow them to be exposed to air, or "breathe."

dessert/sweet wine Wine containing large amounts of sugar. It tastes sweet and is traditionally used to accompany dessert.

disgorgement The traditional process by which the sediment is removed from a bottle of Champagne following the second fermentation.

dosage (French) Term given to the replenishment of the small amount of wine lost during disgorgement in the process of making Champagne. Sugar is also normally added at this stage.

dry-farmed Vines grown without the use of irrigation, thus relying entirely on natural rainfall.

E

en primeur (French) Wine sold by a producer before it has been bottled. Typically customers pay for the wine six months after the harvest, then wait a further 18 months to receive it. This is the best way to secure a wine limited in quantity, but is no guarantee of a cheaper price.

enology (or oenology) The study of wine. The term is principally associated with winemaking.

estate bottled/grown Today, most quality producers bottle on site. It is no guarantee of quality, but is generally a good indicator. In the US, estate bottled wine must also come from the producer's own vineyards or those on a long-term lease. The equivalent in France is *mise en bouteille à la propriété/au domaine/au château*.

F

fermentation The process that turns the juice of crushed, pressed, or whole grapes into wine. The natural sugars within the berries are converted into alcohol and carbon dioxide using yeast. Fermentation generally takes place in stainless steel, lined concrete, or large wooden vats, or in oak barrels. *See also* **malolactic fermentation**.

filtration A technique that removes the tiny solid particles from a wine before bottling, leaving it clear and bright. Some producers believe that filtration can strip a wine of its flavor and will avoid the technique—often including words such as *unfiltered* or *non-filtré* on their label. Wines that have not been filtered will generally require decanting.

fining A process used to remove suspended deposits in wine. When a fining agent such as egg white or bentonite clay is added, it binds with the deposits and causes them to fall to the bottom of the cask.

first growth *See* **premier cru**.

flying winemaker An individual who produces wine in a number of locations around the world. The term was originally coined when highly trained New World winemakers were brought in to revitalize old fashioned, traditional estates in Europe.

fortified A wine bolstered by the addition of a spirit—usually grape spirit—such as port, sherry, or madeira.

French oak A type of wood originating from forests in France such as Allier and Vosges. French oak is widely considered to make the finest barrels for fermenting and maturing wine.

fruit set This is when the fertilized vine flowers become grape berries—not all flowers will actually turn into berries.

fungal diseases A collective term for a number of diseases such as powdery mildew, downy mildew, and black rot. The fungi attack grapes or foliage and, without preventative measures, can cause considerable damage. The benevolent disease *Botrytis cinerea* is also included in this category.

futures The American term for *en primeur*.

G

garage wine A relatively recent term given to the tiny quantities of top quality (and often very expensive) wine made by small-scale producers. Equipment and facilities are generally basic, and production may even take place in a garage, hence the name.

Geographic Indications or **GI** System of labeling wines, based on state and regional boundaries, in use in Australia since 1994.

grand cru (French) Meaning literally "great vineyard." In Burgundy, the term *grand cru* is applied to the finest vineyards in the region. In the St-Émilion area of Bordeaux, the best châteaux are classified as *grand cru classé*, with the top tier known as *premier grand cru classé*. *See also* **premier cru.**

grand vin (French) Often seen on French AOC labels, this literally means "great wine" and is often used to indicate that this is the top wine of a particular estate.

green harvesting The practice of removing and discarding grapes in the build-up to the (conventional) harvest. The idea is to allow the vine to concentrate its energies on ripening the grapes that remain.

H

hybrid A plant created from parents that belong to different species of vine. An example is the Baco Noir grape variety, made by crossing Folle Blanche of the *Vitis vinifera* species with a variety of *Vitis riparia*, a native American species of vine. In the EU, quality wine can only be made entirely from *Vitis vinifera* plants.

IJ

Indicazione Geografica Tipica or **IGT** (Italian) A relatively recent classification for Italian wines, similar to *vin de pays* in France.
jeroboam An oversized bottle containing 3 liters, or four conventional bottles.

KL

late harvest *See vendange tardive.*
lees Known as *lie* in France, lees are the remains of yeast, grape seeds, and other sediment that settle in a wine after fermentation. Extended contact with the lees plays an important role in wines such as Muscadet and Champagne. Lees stirring (*bâtonnage* in French) in cask helps to accentuate this process.
limited release A term used by marketing people on wine labels. It may indicate additional quality, but there is no guarantee.
long-lived This term describes a wine able to develop and improve in bottle over years or decades. Only a small proportion of wines are capable of this. *See also* **ageing**.

M

maceration The practice of soaking grape skins in their juice or must. This gives red wines their color, tannins, and flavors.
madeira A fortified wine produced on the Portuguese island of Madeira.

maderized A wine that has been exposed to oxygen and/or heated to make it taste like madeira. The term is also used occasionally to describe a wine that has been oxidized.
magnum A 1.5 liter bottle (equivalent to two conventional bottles). Wine in a magnum tends to mature more slowly and elegantly than in 75cl bottles and this is believed to be the ideal size for Champagne.
malolactic fermentation A process that converts tart malic acids (as found in apples) into softer lactic acids (as found in milk). It occurs shortly after the first (conventional) fermentation. Most red wines undergo malolactic fermentation; in whites, the decision largely depends on the style of wine the producer is trying to achieve.
Master of Wine or **MW** An extremely demanding wine qualification developed by the Institute of Masters of Wine in London. It covers winemaking, distribution, tasting, and commercial aspects of the industry. There are currently fewer than 250 MWs worldwide.
maturation The process of ageing or maturing a wine in cask or bottle, normally at the winery. Once the wine is released, it may be matured further by the purchaser, but this is more commonly referred to as cellaring or laying down.
Meritage A wine made from the same blend of grape varieties as Bordeaux (Cabernet Sauvignon, Merlot, Cabernet Franc, Malbec, and Petit Verdot for reds; Sauvignon Blanc and Semillon for whites) but from an alternative origin, usually California or South Africa.
méthode champenoise/classique Alternative terms for *méthode traditionnelle.*
méthode traditionnelle (French) Describes a

sparkling wine made using the same techniques as Champagne. In particular, it indicates that the wine has undergone a secondary fermentation in bottle.
monopoly or *monopole* (French) A vineyard completely owned by one individual or organization.
must The mass of grape juice, skins, seeds, stems, and other matter before fermentation begins.
mutage (French) Technical term for the process of halting fermentation before it has naturally finished, normally through the addition of a spirit. The technique is used to create port or *vin doux naturel.*

N

négociant (French) Literally merchant; a person or organization that buys grapes, must, or wine from growers to bottle under its own label. Particularly important in areas with large numbers of small vineyard holdings such as Burgundy. The quality of *négociant* wines can range from poor to excellent.
noble rot *See* **botrytis**.
non-vintage (NV) A blend of wines from different years. Although the term "vintage" is often used to imply high quality, there is nothing inherently wrong with non-vintage wine—indeed most Champagnes are non-vintage.

O

oak The wood favored by winemakers to ferment and mature wines. Many cheaper wines receive their oaky taste from oak chips or oak staves submerged in the tanks. *See also* **American oak**, **French oak**.
oaked A wine made in a deliberately creamy, oaky style through the use of oak barrels, oak chips, or oak staves. *See also* **unoaked**.
old vines *See vieilles vignes.*

organic It is very difficult to produce a completely organic wine as certain chemicals are essential during winemaking. Many wines advertised as such are simply grown without the use of chemical fertilizers, fungicides, and pesticides.

PQ

Pierce's disease A potentially devastating bacterial disease for which there is no known cure. The disease is spread by small insects, known as sharpshooters, and attacks the leaves of the vine. It is most common in the southern part of the US and South America.

phylloxera A vine disease that devastated the vineyards of Europe at the end of the 19th century. Phylloxera is a small insect or aphid that feeds on the roots of grapevines and ultimately kills the plant. Even today there is no cure for the pest—instead almost all European vines are grafted onto rootstocks from American species, which are phylloxera-resistant.

port A sweet, fortified wine produced in the Douro Valley in northern Portugal.

premier cru *(French)* First growth or first vineyard. In the Médoc region of Bordeaux, the finest châteaux are classified as *premier cru*. In St-Émilion just across the river, the top producers are known as *premier grand cru classé*. Confusingly, in Burgundy *premier cru* vineyards lie just below *grand cru* in the classification hierarchy.

R

racking The process of separating a wine from its sediment in the winery. The sediment is normally allowed or encouraged to fall to the bottom of the barrel. The liquid is then drained or pumped into a clean vessel.

raisining The practice of drying grapes either on the vine or after picking. Raisined grapes are normally highly concentrated with sugar, making excellent sweet wines.

reserve A term seen regularly on wine labels to denote a special bottling or release. Unless the wine comes from a reputable producer, however, it is no guarantee of special quality.

residual sugar Sugar that remains in a wine after fermentation. High levels of residual sugar make a wine taste sweet.

rootstock The root system of a vine. Today, almost all vines consist of an American rootstock grafted onto a fruiting European variety to protect against phylloxera.

rosé *(French)* Wine with a pink color, a halfway house between a red and a white wine. The only region allowed to produce rosés by mixing red and white wines is Champagne; the vast majority of other rosés are made using red grapes and a short period of maceration.

ruby port The youngest and fruitiest style of port.

S

sec *(French)* Dry.

sediment Solid matter found in wine. This may come from yeasts, fragments of grape skin and pulp during winemaking, or it may form naturally in the wine. Certain wines "throw" a sediment when matured in bottle for a long period. Such wines will need decanting.

sherry A fortified wine from the Jerez region of Spain.

single vineyard Wine made using grapes from just one vineyard.

stabilization The processes in the winery designed to ensure a wine undergoes no further fermentation or reaction once it is bottled. These include fining and filtration.

structure A tasting term used primarily for red wines to describe the weight of fruit and tannins on the palate. Full-bodied wines such as high quality red Bordeaux should have a "good structure."

T

table wine In theory, the lowest wine classification in the European Union. In general, these wines are cheap and not so cheerful. However, some of Europe's finest wines are labeled "table wine." Price is a good guide to quality here—finer wines in this category tend to cost significantly more than basic table wine.

tannins The astringent, mouth-drying compounds found when a teabag is soaked in water too long. Tannins in grapes are found in the skins, seeds, and stalks, and are particularly important in the composition of a red wine. They provide the wine with its structure and weight and also act as a preservative, helping it to mature in bottle. A wine with excessive tannins is described as "tannic."

tawny port A style of port characterized by its distinctive tawny color. Better examples achieve their appearance and soft, mellow taste through extended maturation in cask.

terroir A French word used to describe the full growing environment of a vineyard, covering its climate, soil, slope, and exposure, among other factors. Advocates of *terroir* believe that a wine should not simply taste of fermented grape juice, but rather it should express a sense of the place where the grapes are grown.

traditional method *See* **méthode traditionnelle**.

U

unfiltered/non-filtré *See* **filtration**.

unoaked A wine deliberately made without oak barrels to emphasize its fresh fruit flavors.

V

varietal A wine that has been labeled on the basis of its principal grape variety. It can also be used as another word for "grape variety."

vendange tardive (French) A French term meaning late harvest. Grapes that have been harvested later tend to be riper and more concentrated, producing sweeter styles of wine. In Alsace, the term carries a legal definition, elsewhere, it can be used simply at the discretion of the producer.

vieilles vignes (French) Literally "old vines." As a vine gets older, it tends to produce fewer, but better quality grapes. It is no guarantee of a superior wine, as there is no legal definition of what constitutes old.

vin de pays (French) Often excellent value, "country wines" sit between table wines and *appellation contrôlée* wines in the classification hierarchy.

vin de table (French) See **table wine**.

vin nouveau (French) See **vin primeur**.

vin primeur (French) Young wine made to be drunk in the same year that it is produced, the best-known example being Beaujolais Nouveau.

vine density The number of vines planted in a specified area in a vineyard. High density planting (around 20,000 vines per acre [8,000 vines per hectare]) is practiced in many European vineyards, as the competition between plants is believed to help lower yields and produce better quality grapes.

vine pull The removal of vines. In parts of Europe where overproduction is a problem, governments pay growers to pull up their vines in vine pull schemes.

vinification Essentially, "winemaking," the process that converts grape juice into finished wine.

vin santo (Italian) A dessert wine made in Tuscany from grapes dried on racks. The wine must be matured in casks for at least three years.

vintage Can be used to mean either "harvest" or the year in which the grapes were grown to produce a wine. A vintage wine must come from a single year. Vintage Champagne is only produced in exceptional years and must be matured for at least three years on its lees. See also **non-vintage**.

vintage port The very best port made from a single fine harvest and aged in wood for around two years. It is "declared" or released by producers only in the best vintages, on average three times a decade.

viticulture Vine growing—the science, techniques, and skills required to produce commercial-quality grapes.

Vitis vinifera The species of vine responsible for the majority of the world's wine.

W

wooded/unwooded See **oaked** and **unoaked**

XYZ

yeast A single-cell fungus that converts sugar into alcohol during fermentation. In many regions, yeasts occur naturally on the skins of grapes and in the air. Many local winemakers prefer these "wild" strains, although cultured yeasts are often more reliable.

yield The total amount of wine produced by a vine or vineyard in a particular vintage. As a rule of thumb, lower yields will produce better quality grapes, and in European appellations, maximum yields are prescribed by law. These will range from around 400 gallons per acre (38 hectoliters per hectare) for *grand cru* red Burgundy to over 1,050 gallons per acre (100 hectoliters per hectare) for the less illustrious classifications.

Index

Index

Acknowledgments

AUTHORS
Top 10 lists by Vincent Gasnier
(see p7). Other text by Ruth
Arnold, Paul Hines, Richard Jones,
Susan Keevil, Jeni Port

BLUE ISLAND PUBLISHING
Editorial Director
Rosalyn Thiro
Art Director
Stephen Bere
Senior Editor
Ferdie McDonald
Associate Editor
Michael Ellis
Designer
Ian Midson
Editorial Researcher
Paul Hines
Picture Researcher
Helen Stallion

DORLING KINDERSLEY
Senior Editor
Janet Mohun
US Senior Editor
Jennifer Williams
Americanization Editor
Jenny Siklos
Senior Art Editor
Helen Spencer
DTP Designer
Traci Salter
Picture Researcher
Romaine Werblow
Production Controller
Mandy Inness
Executive Managing Editor
Adèle Hayward
Managing Art Editor
Karla Jennings

PICTURE CREDITS
The publishers would like to thank
all the wine producers and picture
libraries for their kind permission
to reproduce their photographs.

AUSTRALIAN WINE AND
BRANDY CORPORATION:
14, 20–21, 24, 26, 29, 31, 42–3,
64–5, 69, 78, 88–9, 98.

CEPHAS: Andy Christodolo 34, 46,
91; Jeffery Drewitz 32–3, 54–5;
Kevin Judd 1, 23, 28, 30, 76–7,
110–111, 115, 116–17; Mick Rock
18, 22, 40.

CORBIS: Charles O'Rear 12, 13.

Courtesy of Jansz Tasmania: 87

Reproduced with the permission
of McWilliam's Wines: 47
(bottom); Barwang Vineyard,
Hilltops NSW, Photographer:
Richard Humphrys. © McWilliam's
Wines Pty Ltd 48, 50.

DK Special Editions
DK books can be purchased in
bulk quantities at discounted
prices for use in promotions or as
premiums. We are also able to
offer special editions and
personalized jackets, corporate
imprints, and excerpts from all of
our books, tailored to meet your
own needs.

To find out more, please contact:
Special Markets Department,
DK Publishing, 375 Hudson Street,
New York, NY 10014